I0803024

FOR NOW

Just look.

Lift your head
and look up and out.
See the tangle of trees,
roots holding the hill
in place,
branches showing off,
stirring the air
like whisks.

For Now

Poems by Taiju Geri Wilimek

Paintings by Marley Kaul

Mill Studio Press

Published by Mill Studio Press
4111 Mill Street NE
Bemidji, MN 56601
www.marleykaul.com
millstudiopress@midco.net

Published in the United States of America

Printed on acid-free, archival-quality paper by CG Book Printers, Mankato, Minnesota

Edited by Kathleen Weflen
Cover and interior design by Lynn Phelps

ISBN: 978-1-7323894-2-7

1. Art. 2. Poetry. 3. Egg Tempera. 4. Zen.
Library of Congress Control Number: 2020919605

FIRST EDITION

Kaul, Marley, 1939–
Wilimek, Taiju Geri, 1953–
For Now/Poems by Taiju Geri Wilimek, Paintings by Marley Kaul

For ***Sandy Kaul,*** my life partner of 58 years, who was instrumental in completing this book. She has carefully attended to the book's process and inspires me in so many ways.

—Marley Kaul

For my daughters, *Jessie* and *Allison*. Of the wonderful women in my life, you are the most precious.

—Geri Wilimek

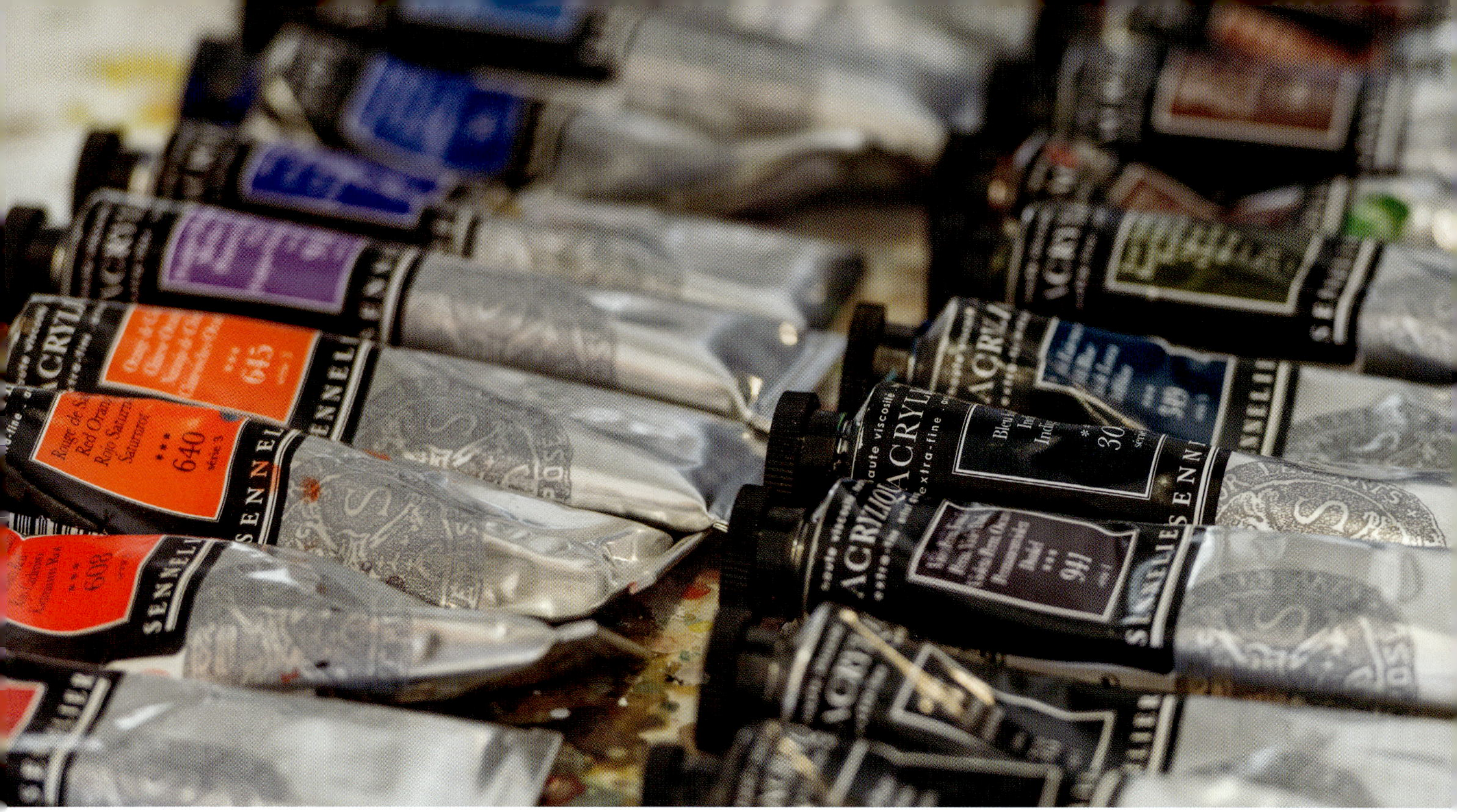

Matthew McLaughl

Foreword

Two mature artists, painter and poet, creating their work independently, have collaborated to produce this book, *For Now*. A master of his craft, Marley Kaul brings his egg tempera paintings into conversation with the haiku-like poems of Zen practitioner Taiju Geri Wilimek. This volume continues the interplay of their first coproduced book, *We Sit*.

The relationship of these paintings and poems is meant to be as random and free-flowing as a conversation. The poems do not serve as captions to the paintings. Nor do the paintings illustrate the poems. Paired on these pages, painting and poem can be read like a kind of daily horoscope suggesting possibilities for today, for now.

Kaul's painting of a wedge of pie and two coffee cups suggests an exchange—the beginning of a conversation. It focuses on a common scene, casting familiar things in a certain light. The viewer comes to the table, pauses, listens, gives attention—even reverence—to this ordinary moment.

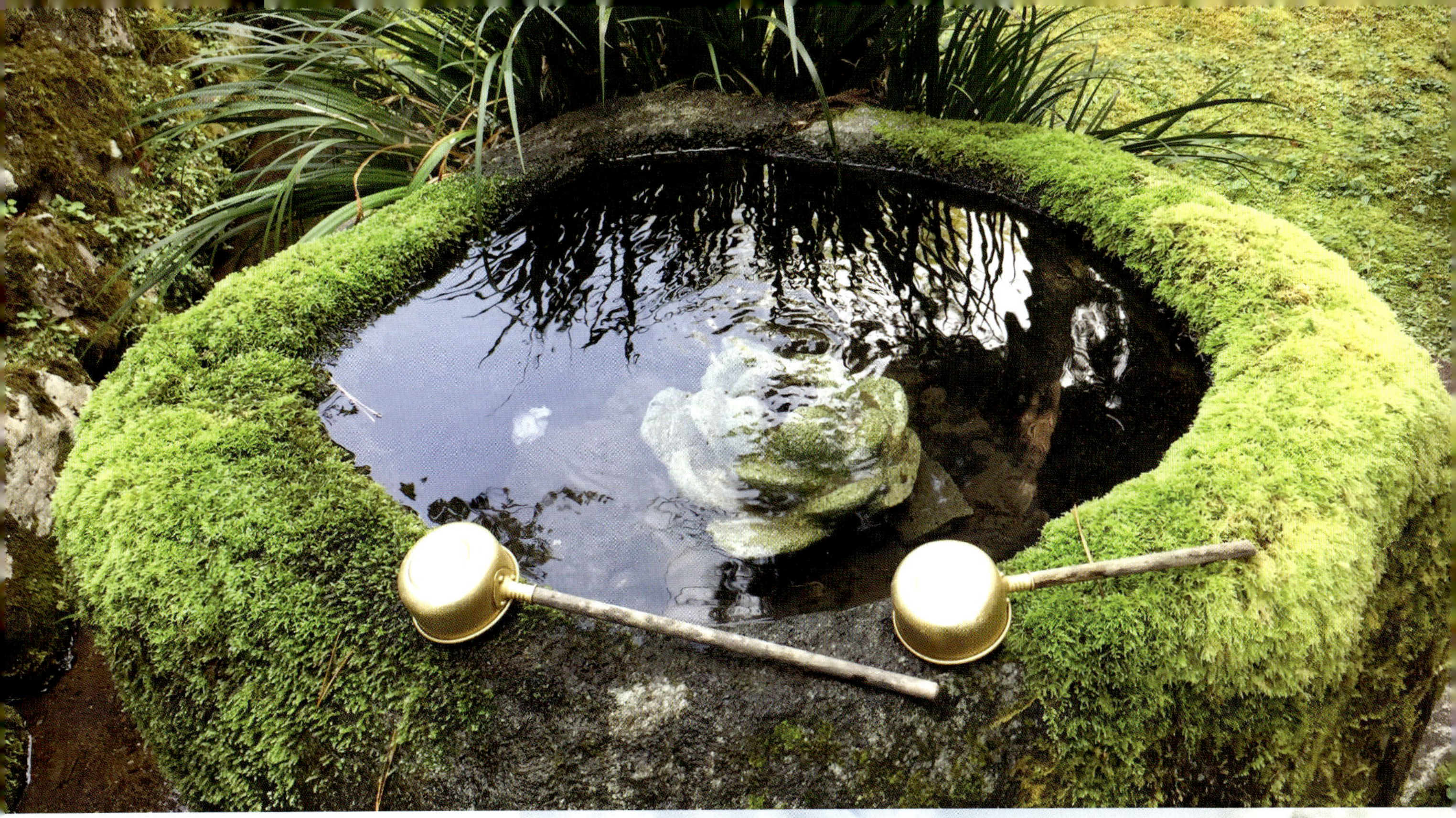

Wilimek too invites the reader to pause in the midst of an ordinary day, in recognition of something familiar. The poems beckon us to notice, to linger on the threshold of awareness, and, in her words, to melt.

The art of *For Now* renders experiences of being human and encourages us to find meaning there.

—*Kathleen Weflen*

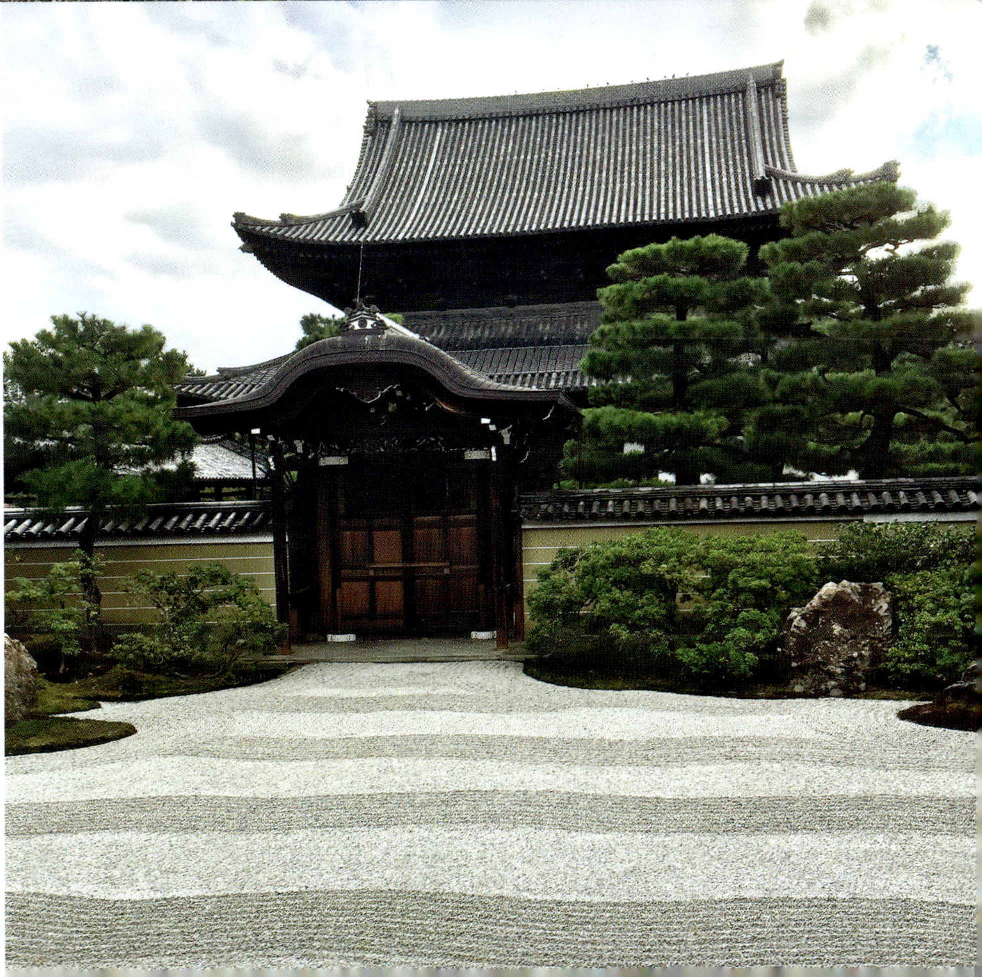

PHOTOS COURTESY OF GERI WILIMEK

First Bouquet

2020

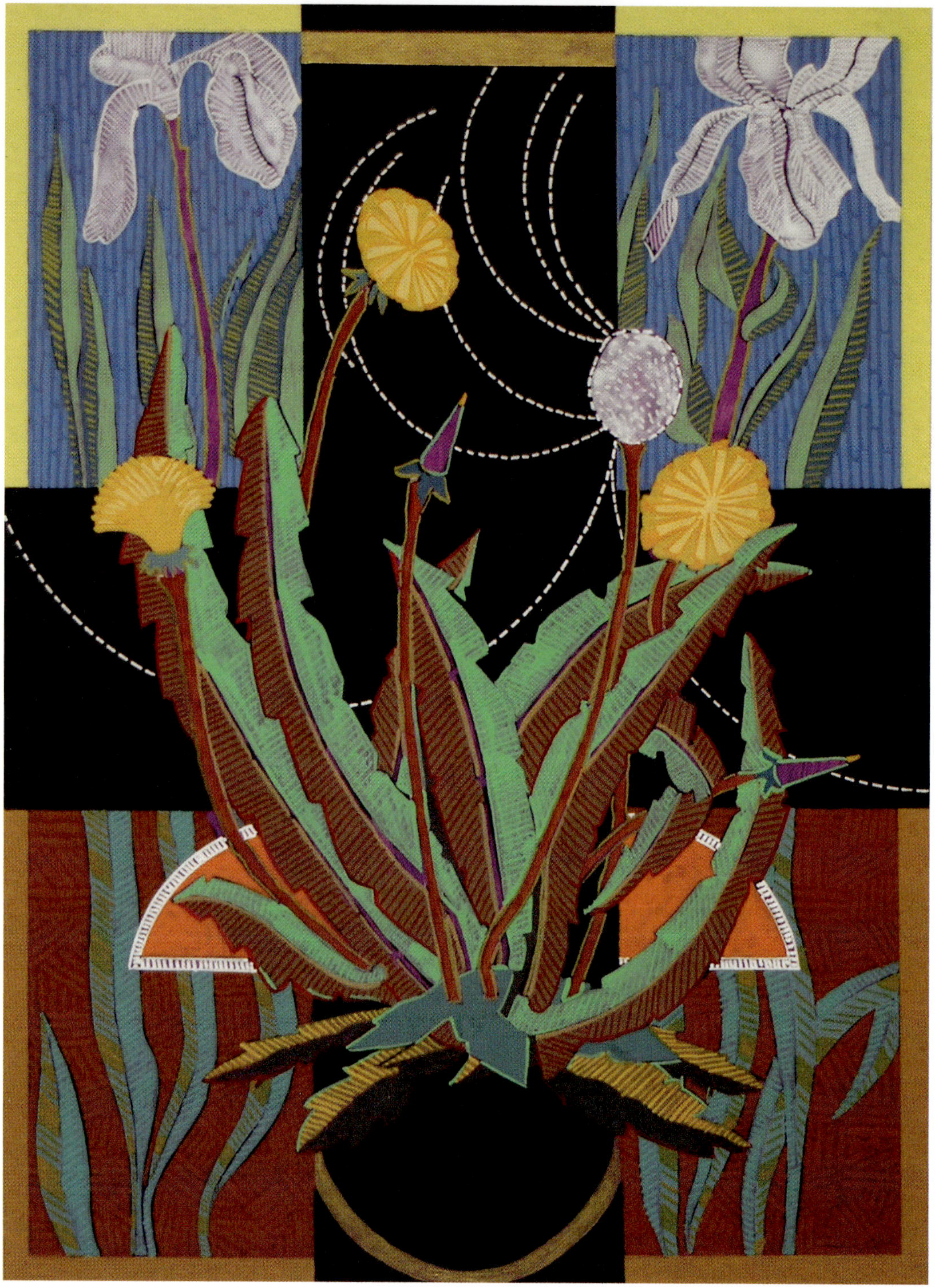

Long after dark

the garden is

held with all things

between cool moon and

radiant earth.

Petals Drop Like Tears

2020

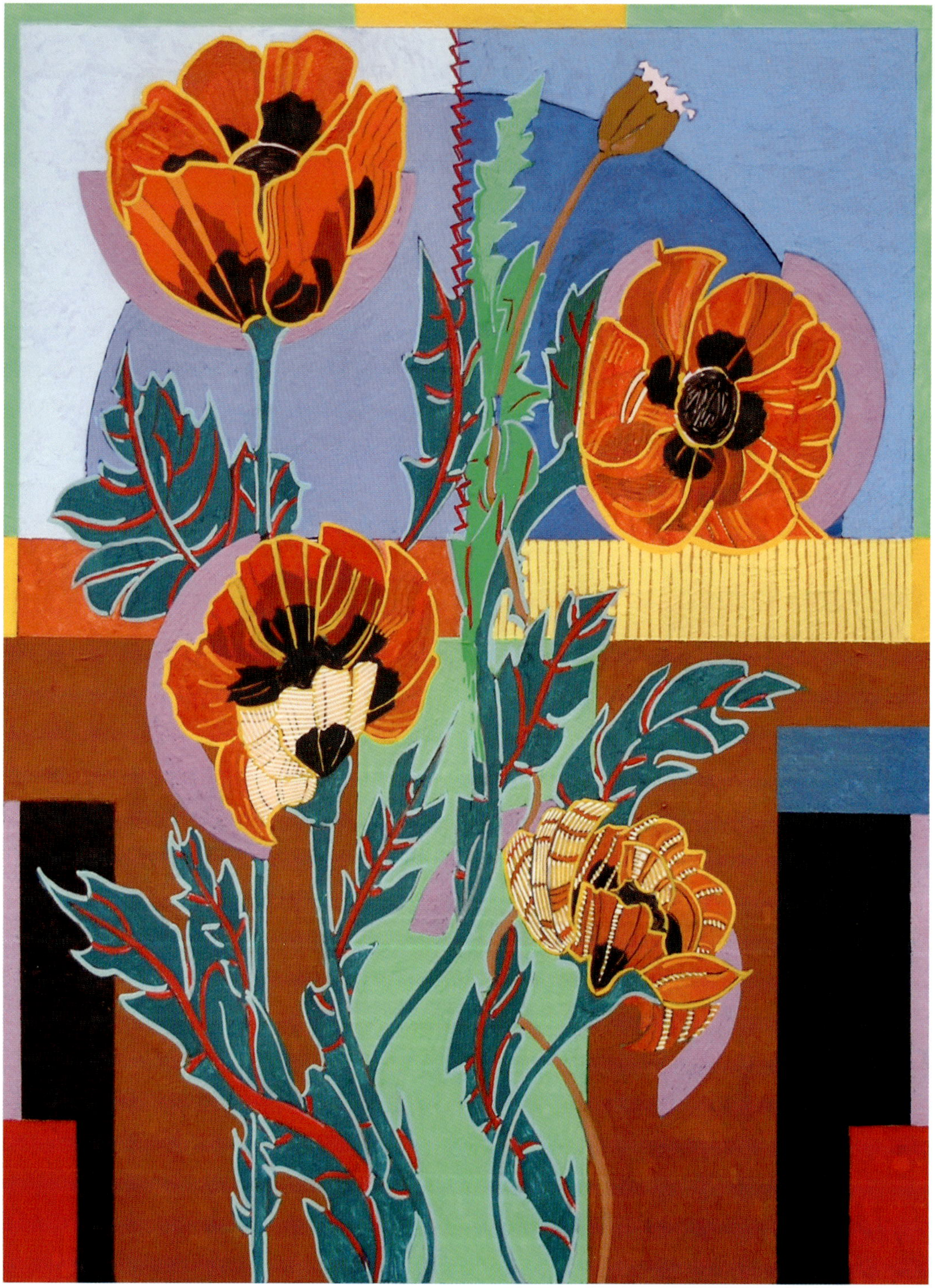

Seeing beyond the blossom,

if you are not careful,

can become the next

episode of desire.

Evening Tea

2018

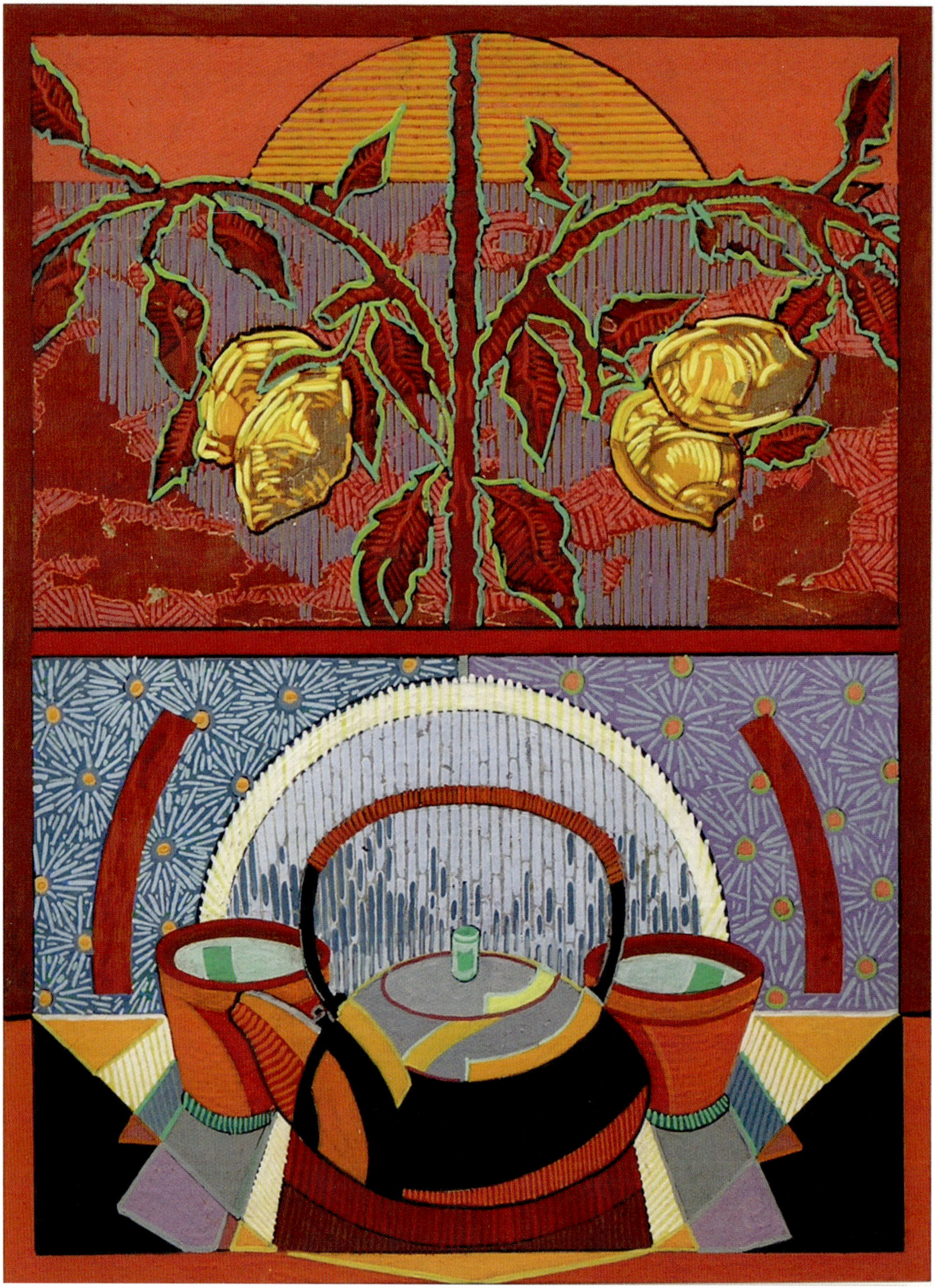

Split,
split open,
abundance
swelling within,
joining the ranks
of all good snakes,
butterflies and
fast ripening
tomatoes.

Silent Echo

2019

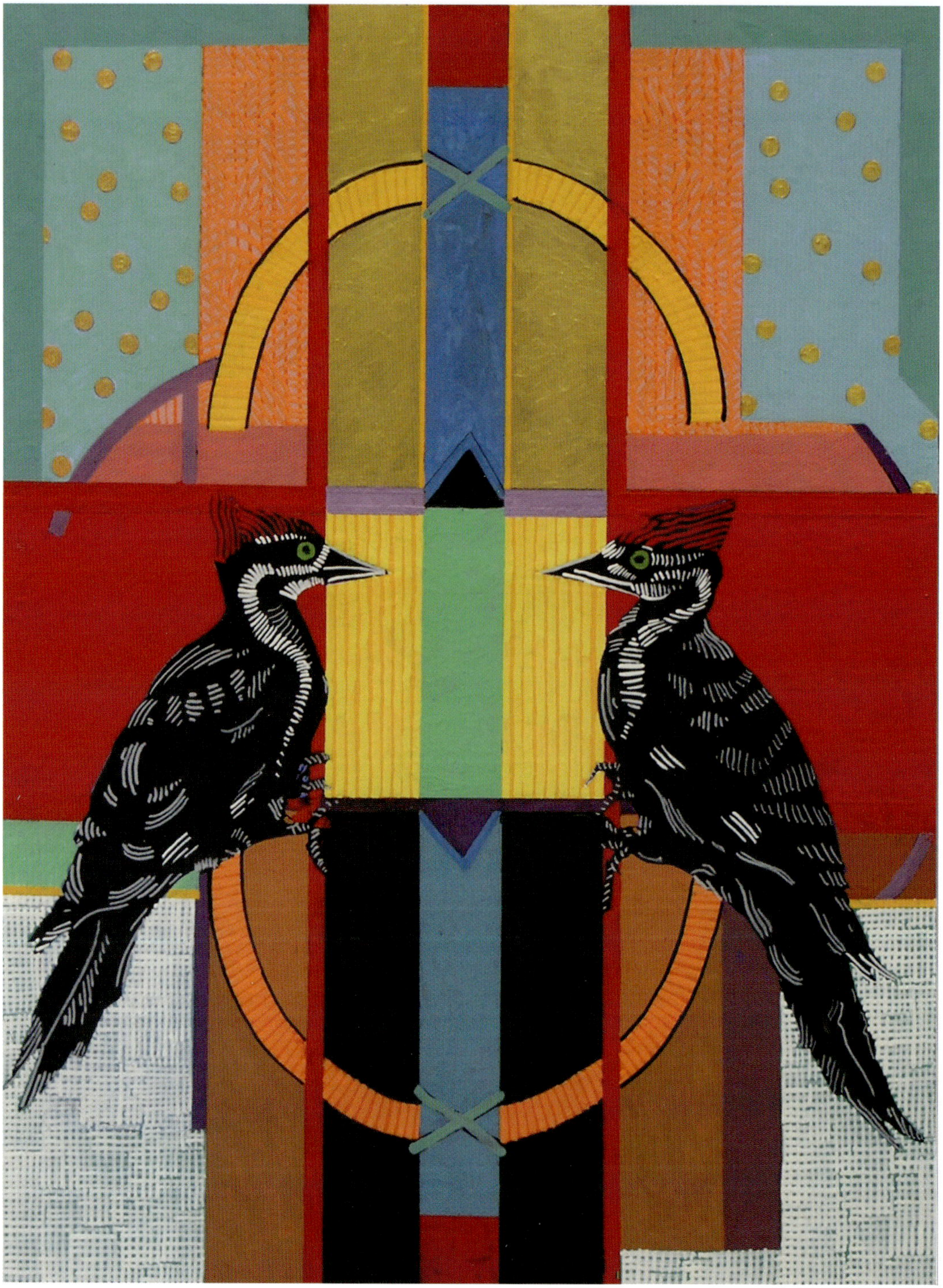

Life seems

gauzy, flexible,
even flimsy,
yet strangely
difficult to tear.

Sitting still now,
there are no problems.

Just waiting for
the parting of threads,
a way through.

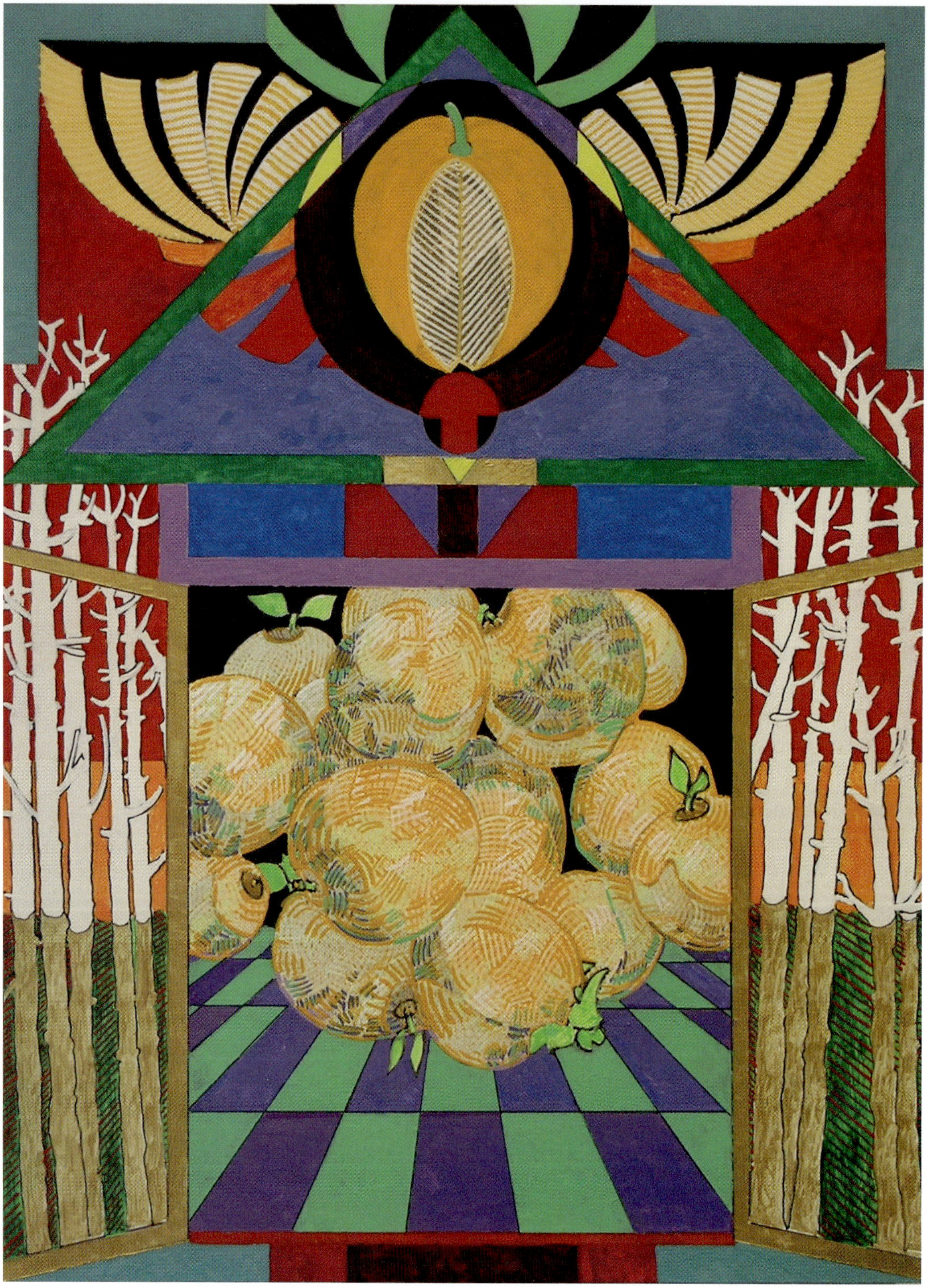

A Myth Revisited

2020

It must have come
from a shiny black throat,
through icy morning air.
It must have penetrated
triple-pane windows,
blankets and sleep,
this awakening
caw.

Yves Blue

2020

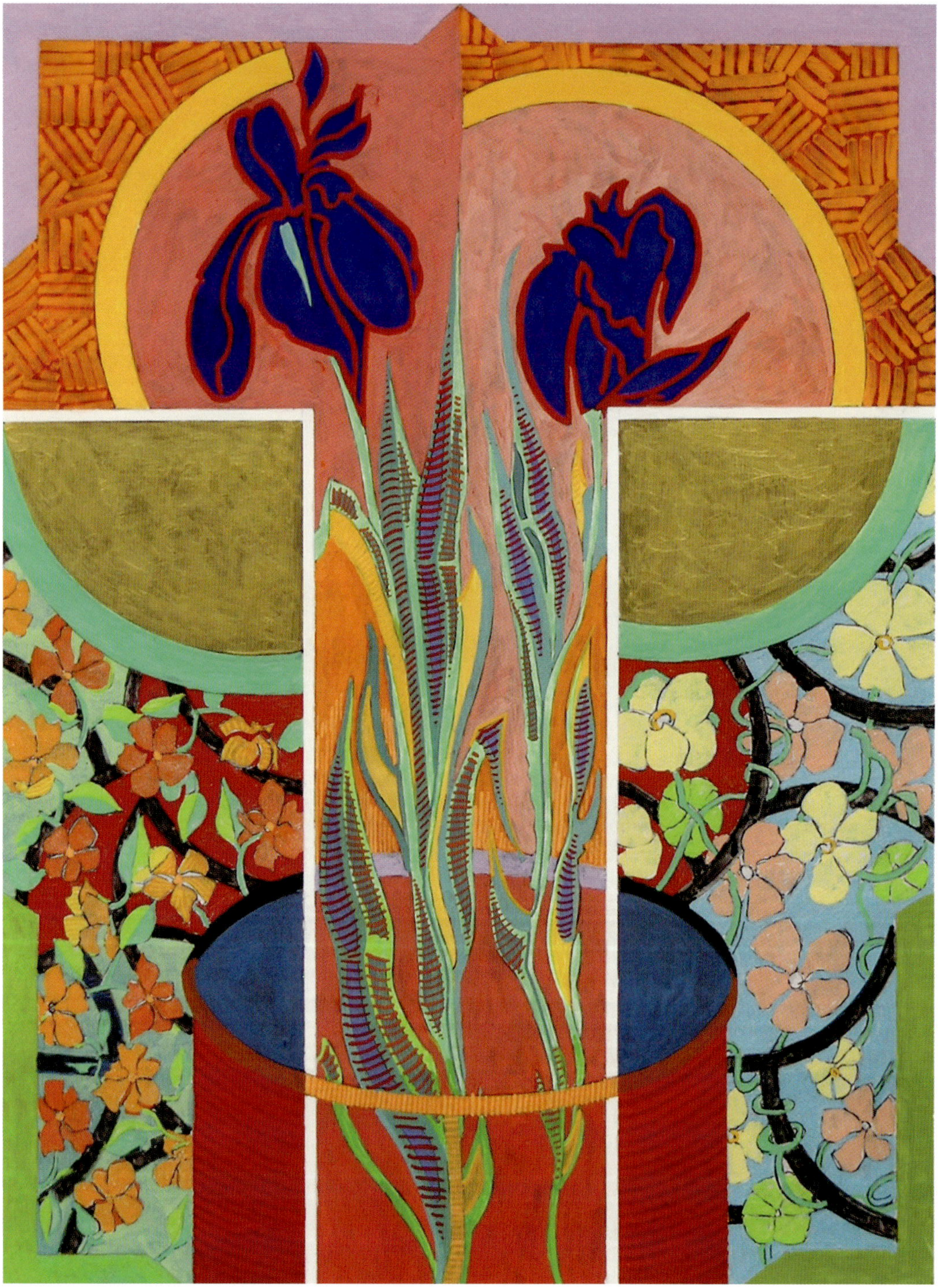

Faint rumbles

yellow sky
dripping eaves
and just now,
a thread
of birdsong
coaxing me out
of this afternoon nap.

ROWAN TREE

2019

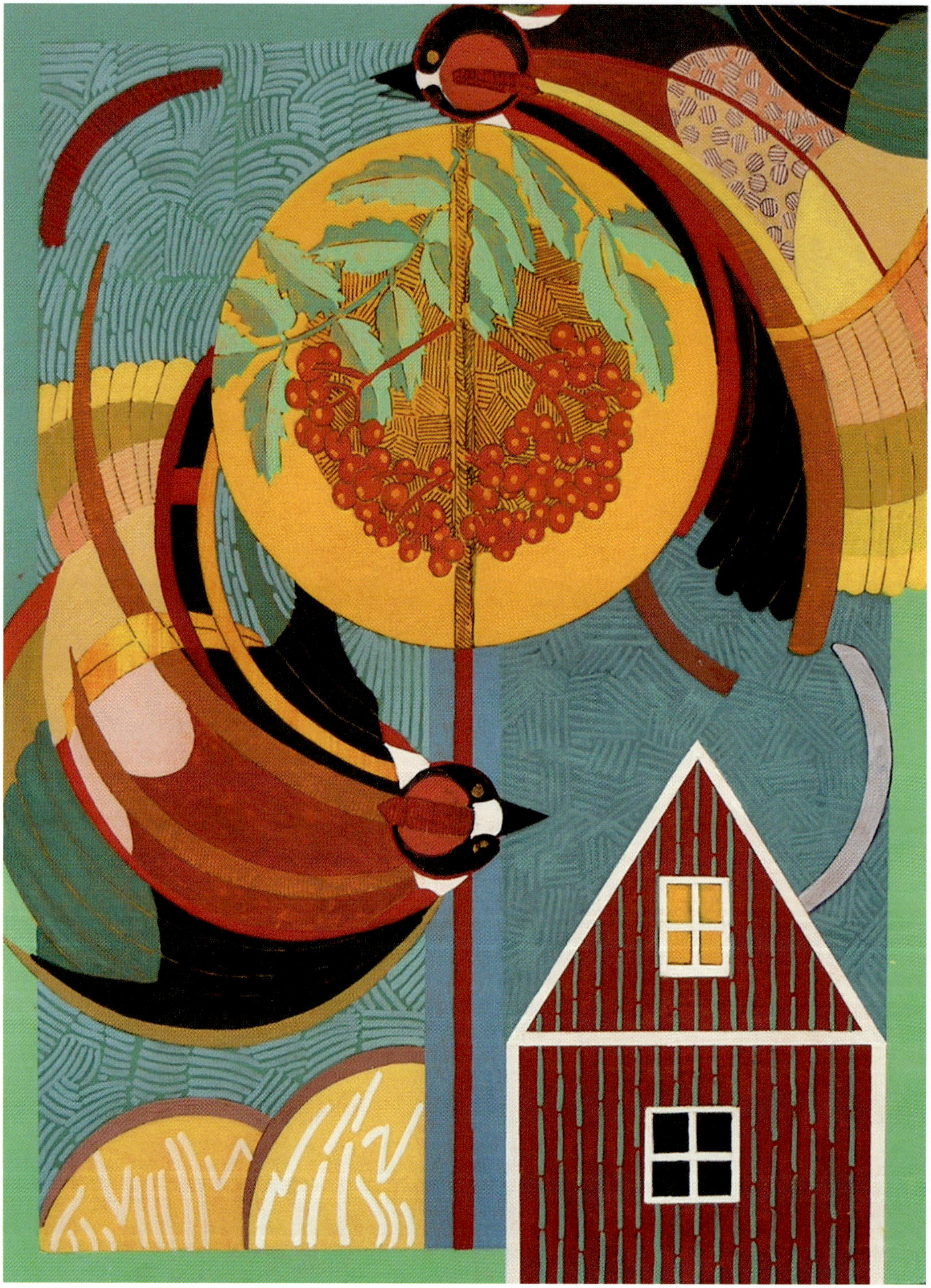

We are here briefly
and brightly.
It matters that we are
connected by invisible lines
earthly constellations,
while ten thousand things
undulate and swirl.

Prune d'Ente

2020

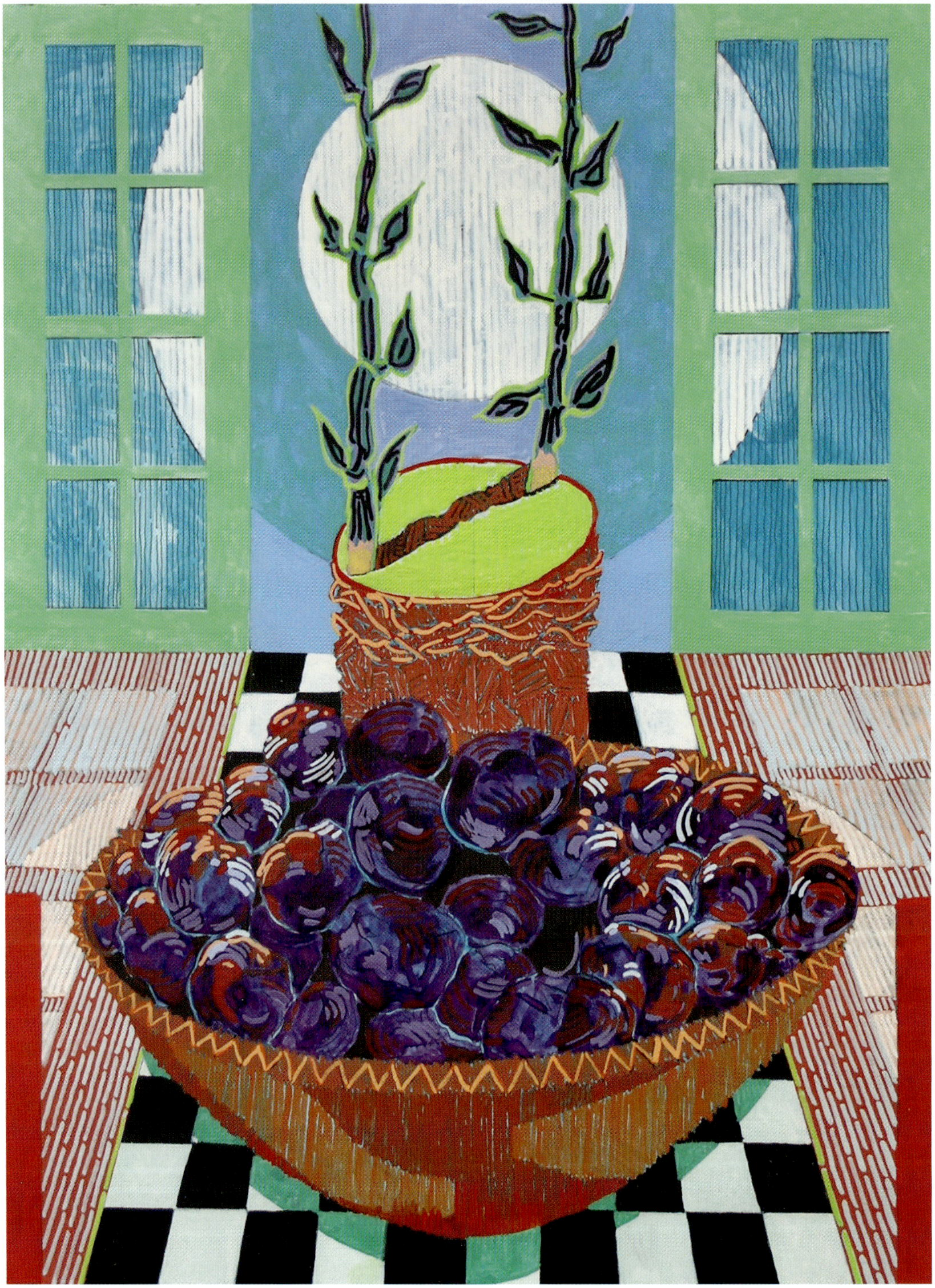

Dousing

these artificial lights
to hear more vividly
loons calling from the
pink waters.
The dog barks madly
at something roaming
in the darkening
woods.

Caught and Redirected

2017

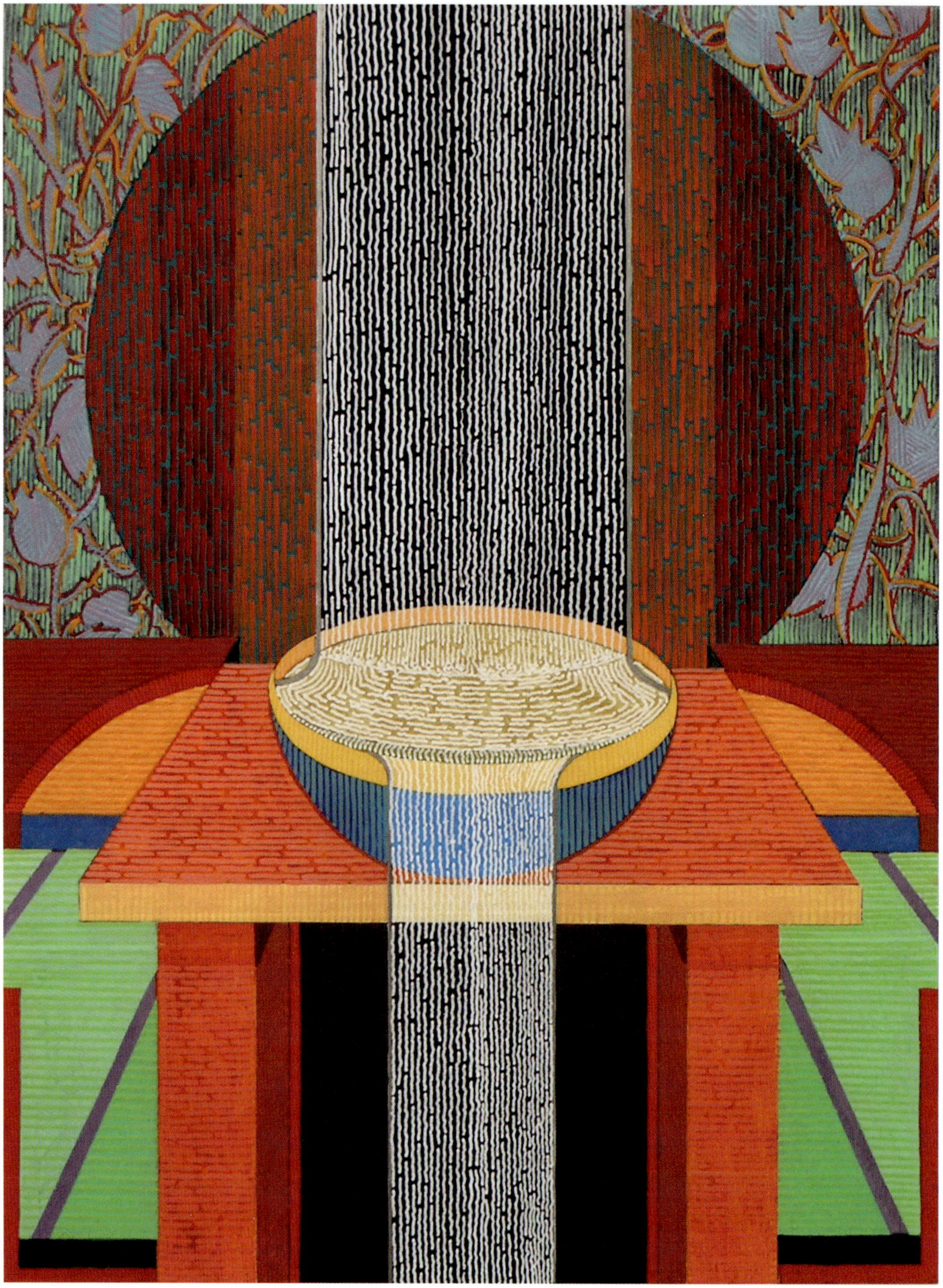

notice

linger

soften

melt

repeat

First Cup

2018

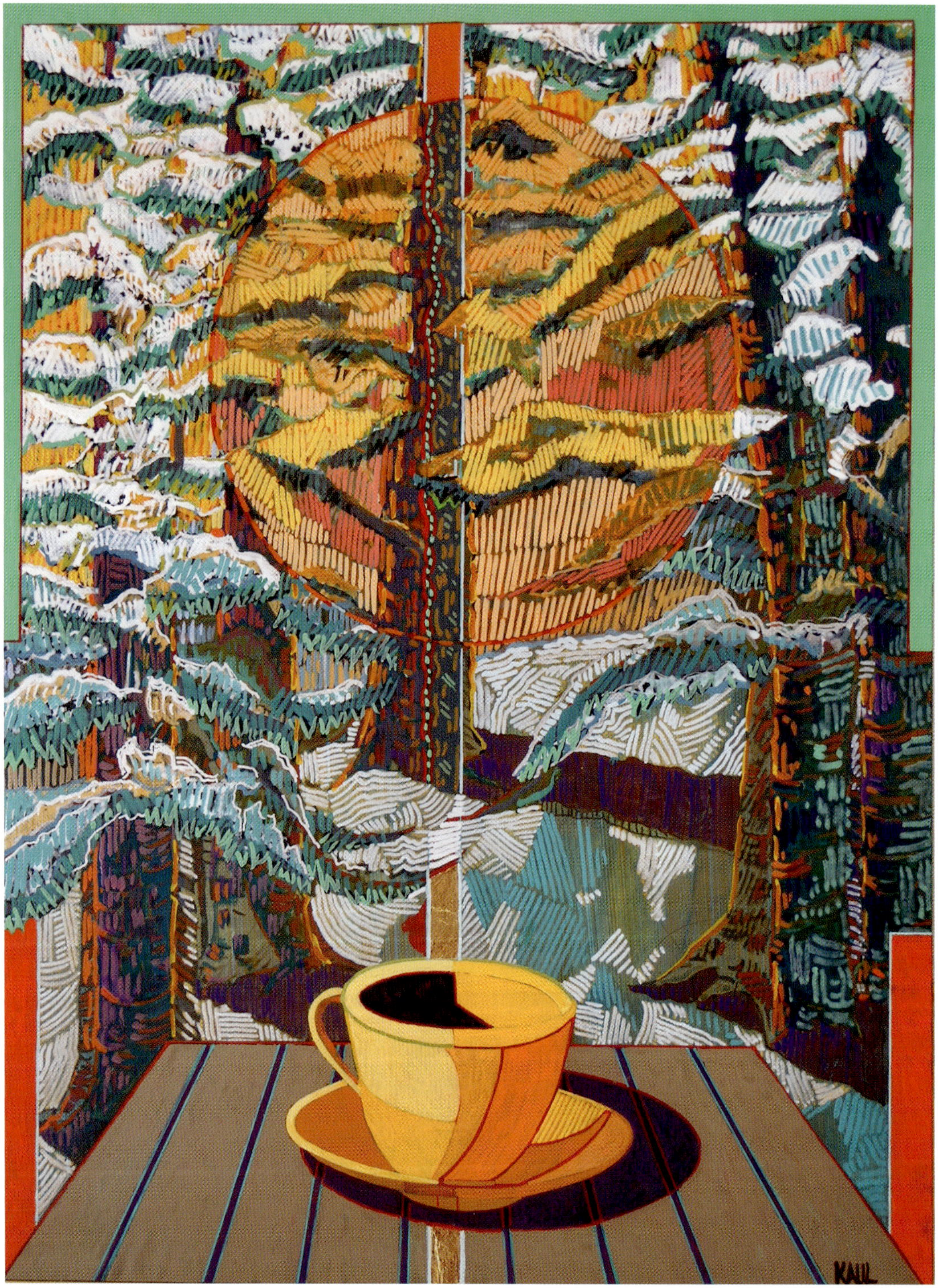

Embedded

within this day,

no stopping or starting.

Attuned to sunlight,

the blaze softened

they say, by

ninety-three

million

miles.

Lift

2019

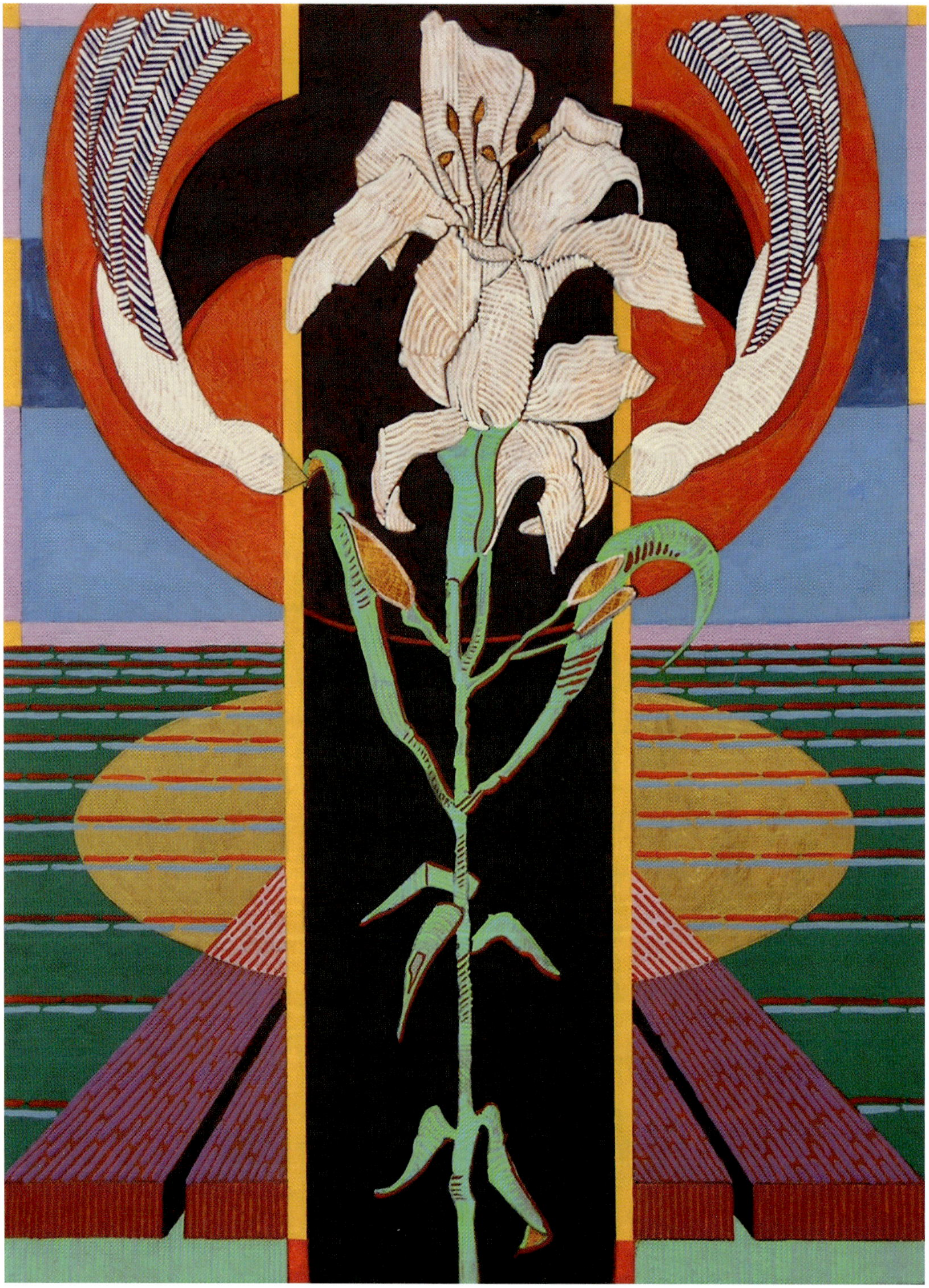

I hope to bear

this as you have borne it.

It is my final exam,

my honor,

my deepest vow.

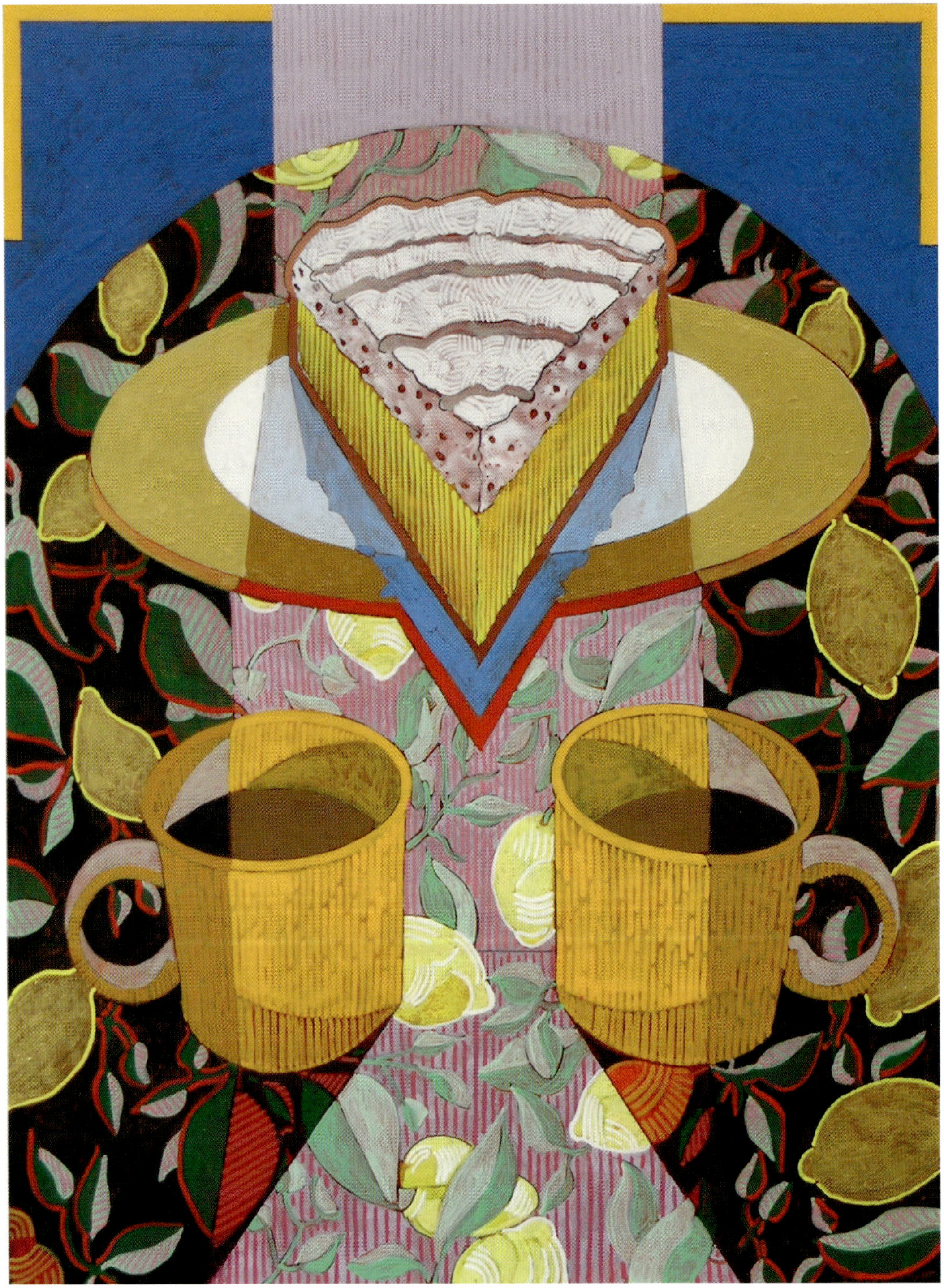

Invitation to Listen

2020

Two chairs
by the cold firepit
angled toward one another
seem friendly and
perfectly at ease
unoccupied.

Cycle of Light

2020

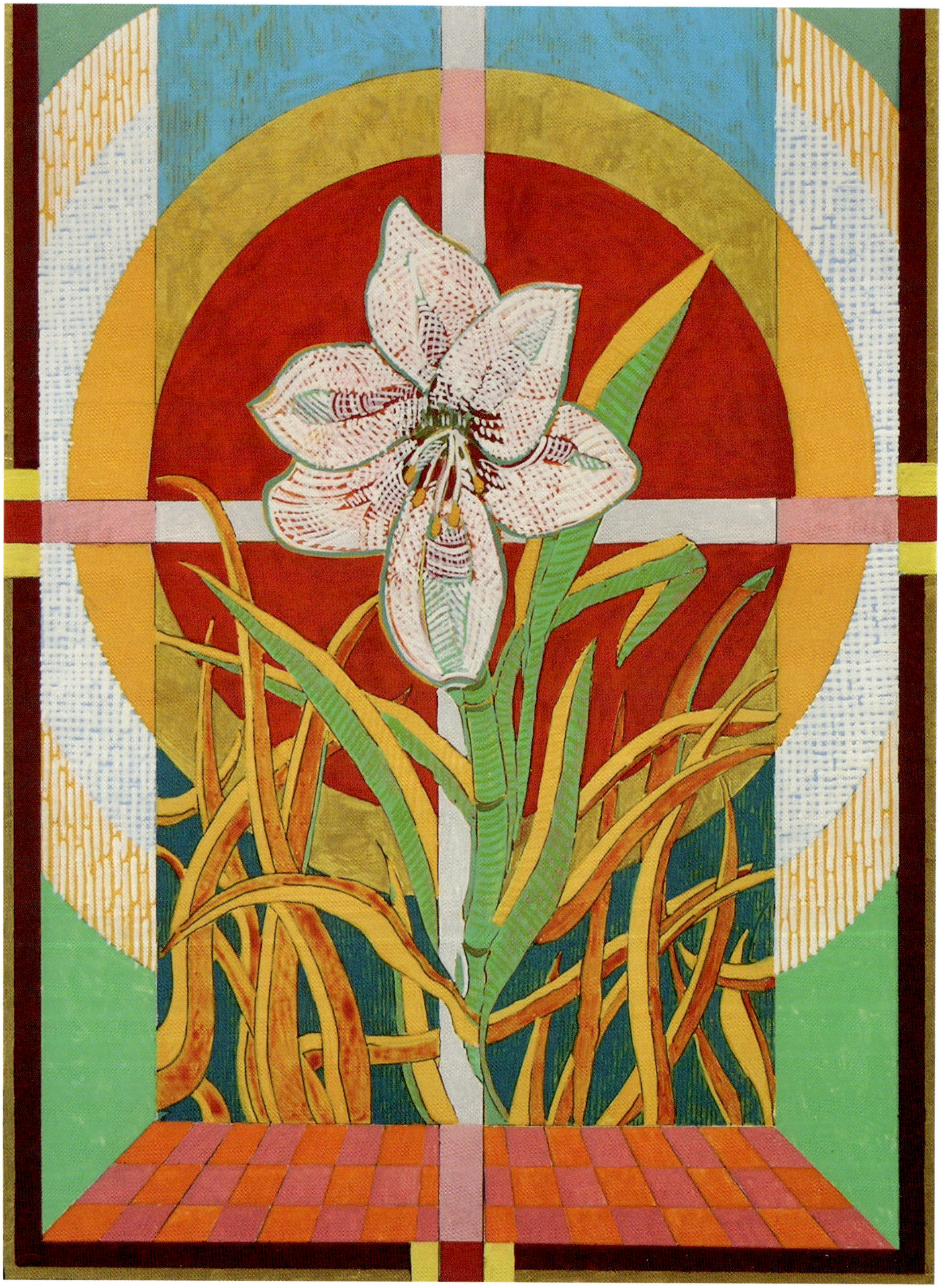

When the obvious
offers an invitation
into itself,
opens a window
shares fresh scents
and deep space,
there is nothing
to do but stop
and gaze,
letting the breeze
into those
layers beneath
the skin.

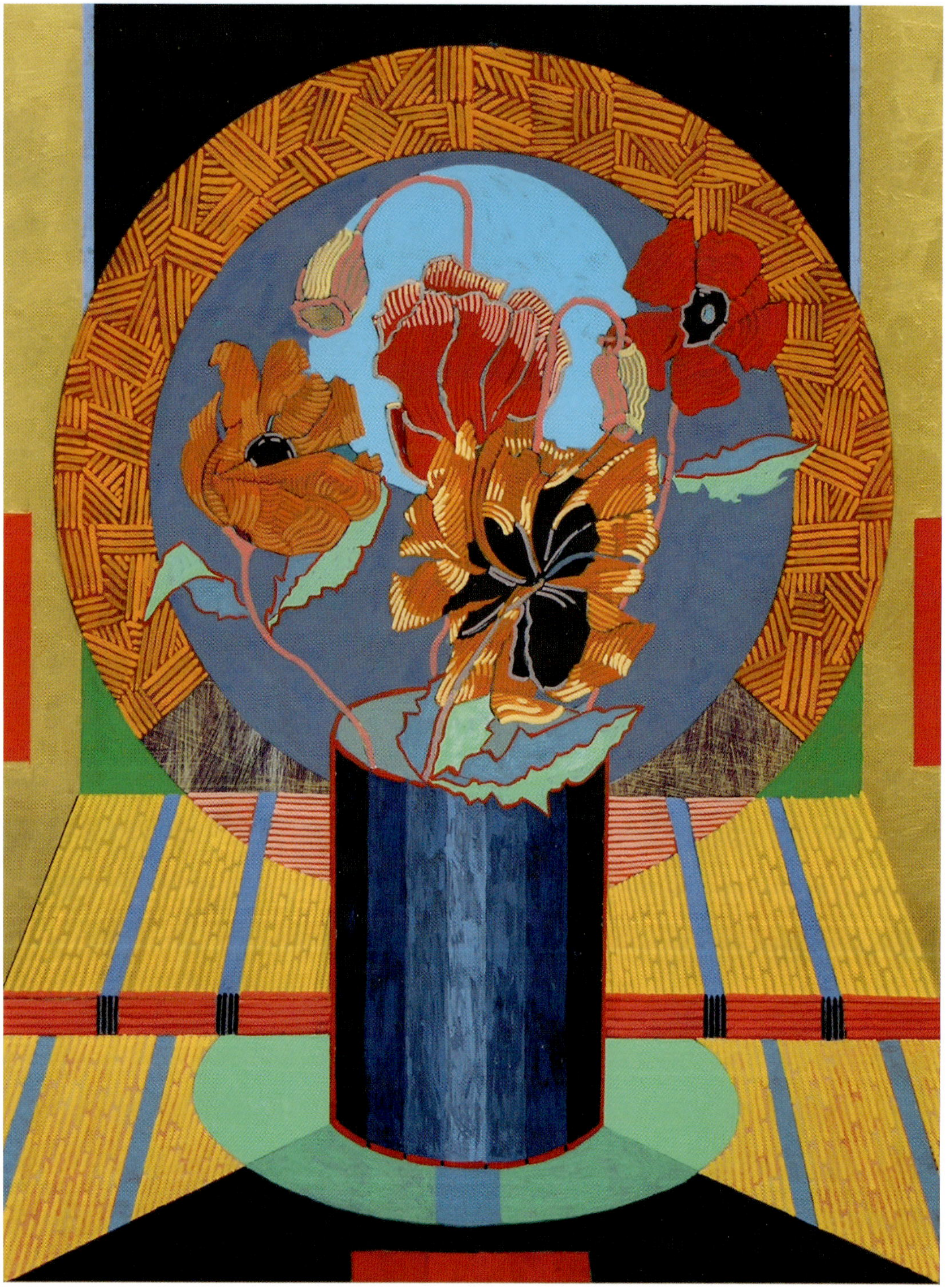

As It Happens

2020

No moon.
Just night, as
empty and rich
as the eye's pupil.

Grief Released

2020

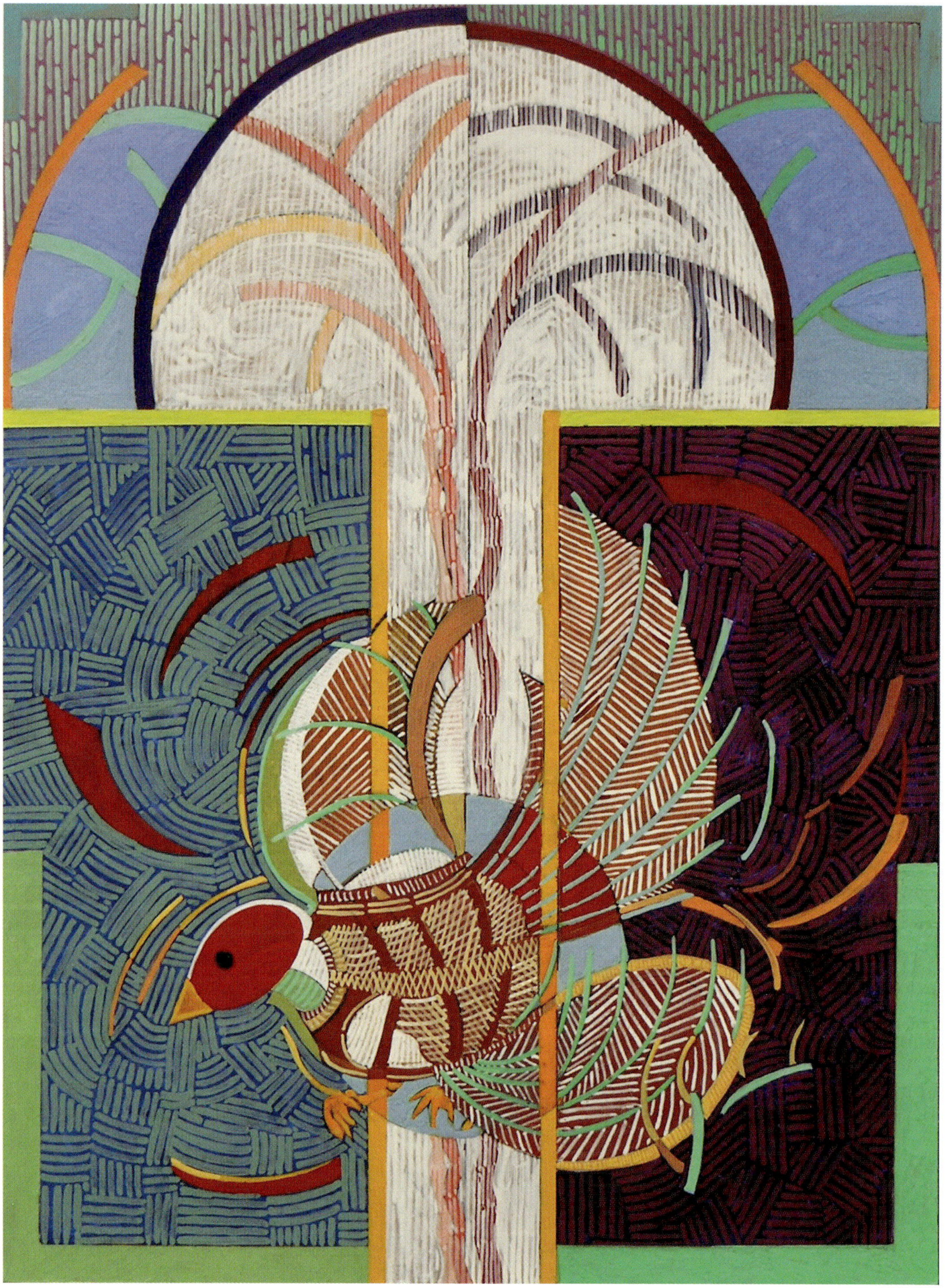

You'll never believe it
when I tell about the bird that
dropped from the sky mid-flight
and landed dead at my feet,
let alone that it turned me
into something
else.

Antrim Whites

2020

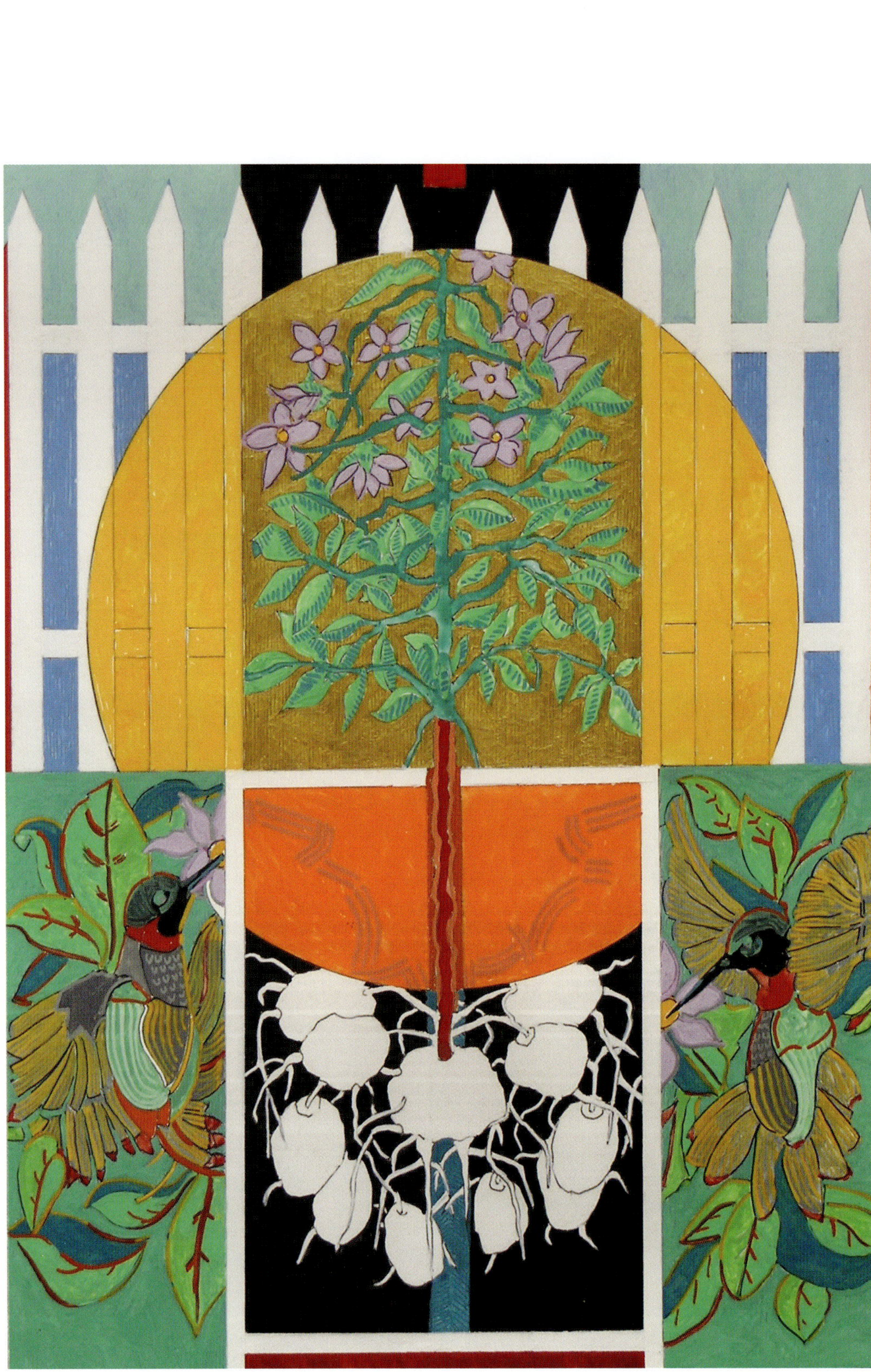

Glowing ember
descends a
stick of incense
on its way to a
bed of fine ash.
I watch as time
goes up in
smoke.

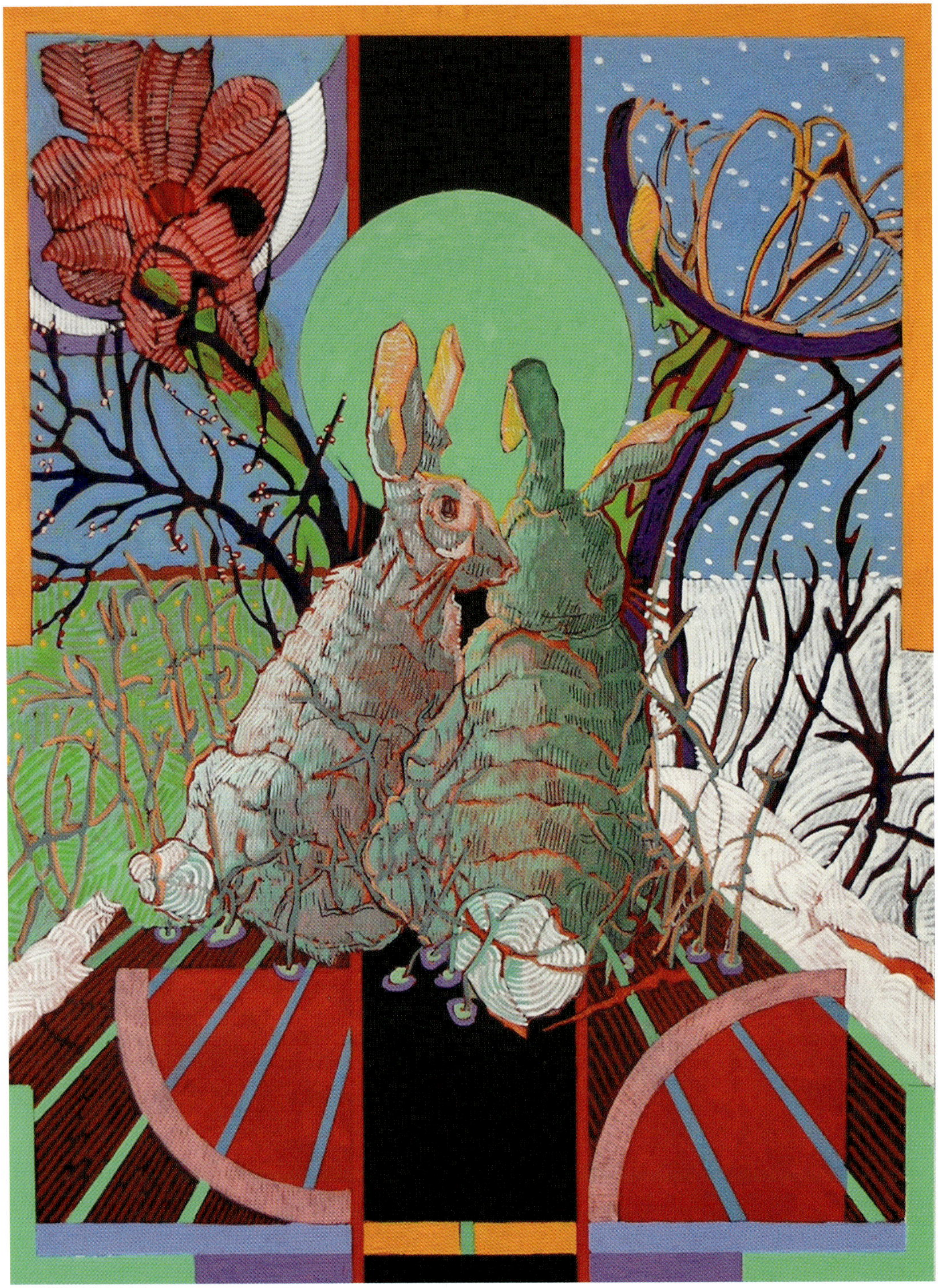

JADE MOON

2019

Joy and Sorrow
arrive uninvited
on the front porch,
often arm in arm,
bearing nothing
but themselves
as gifts.

The Dance

2020

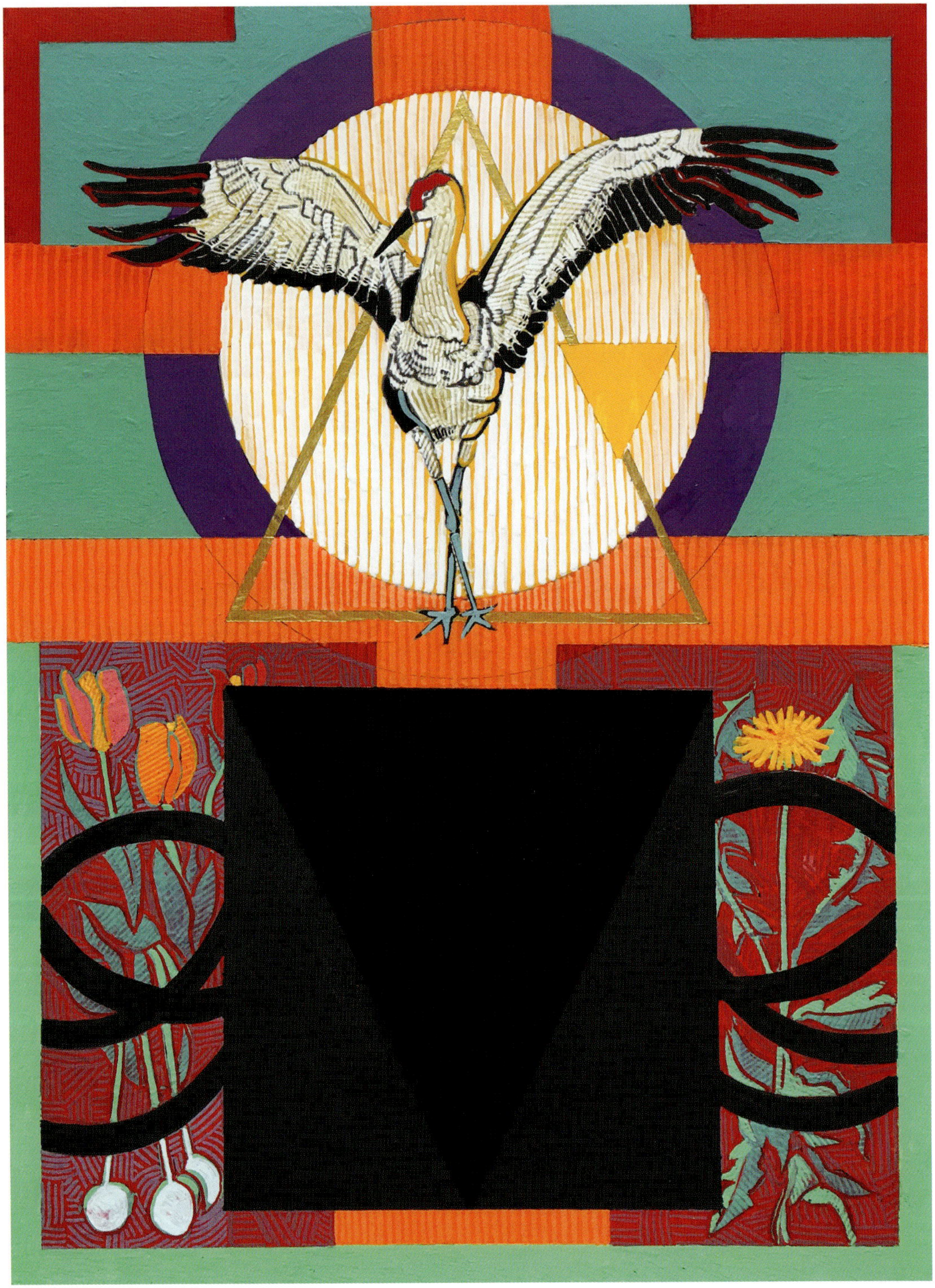

It isn't
at all like I thought.
It isn't like anything
ever known in body or mind,
this moment melding with
all beings: past, present, future,
shedding every last thing
that made us
differ.

Bramble Dome

2018

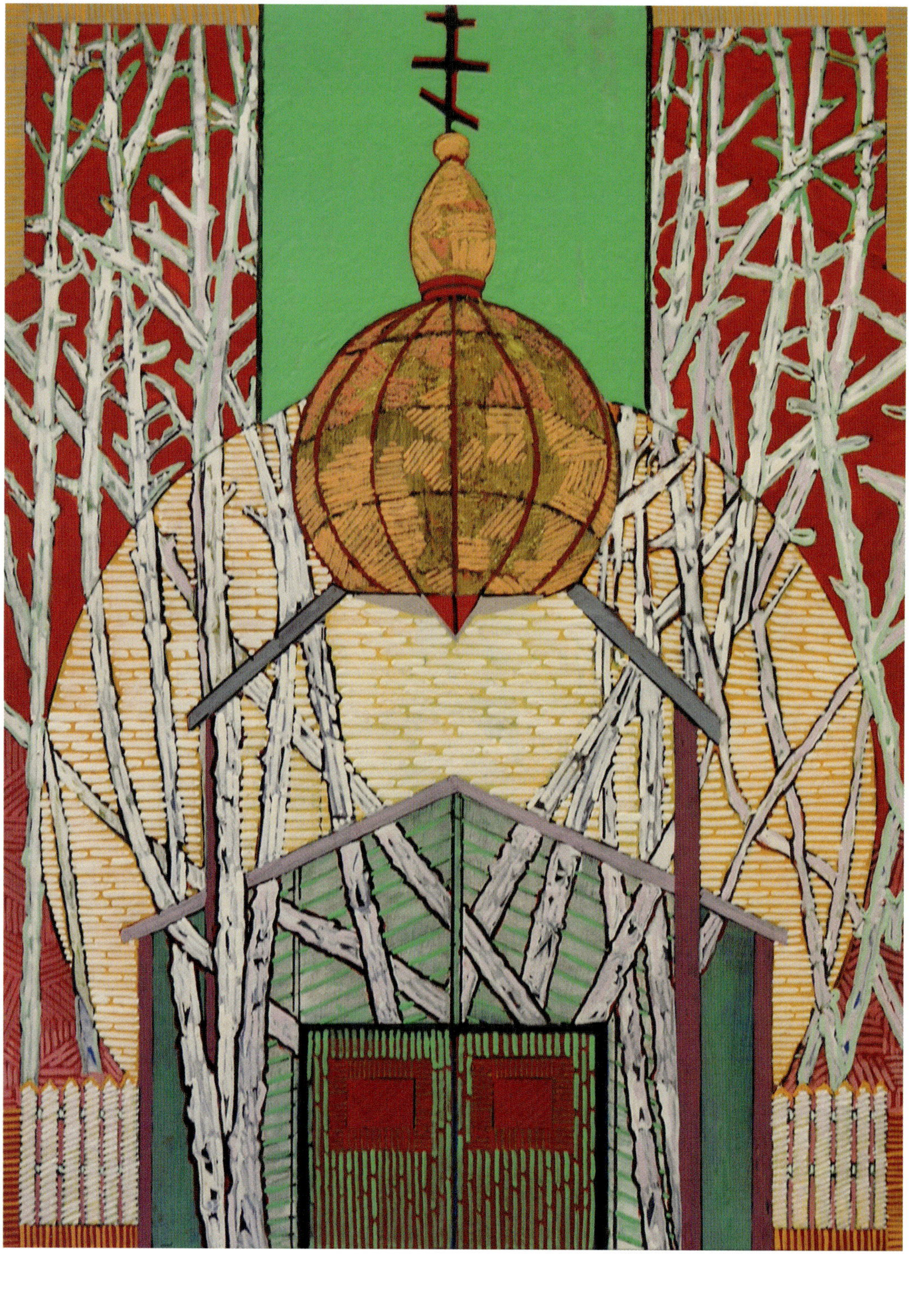

Little ham buns
piled high on a platter,
nothing more than
smokey salt and butter
tucked into
soft, sweet bread,
the allowable pleasure
we call comfort on this
somber occasion.

Companion Planting

2020

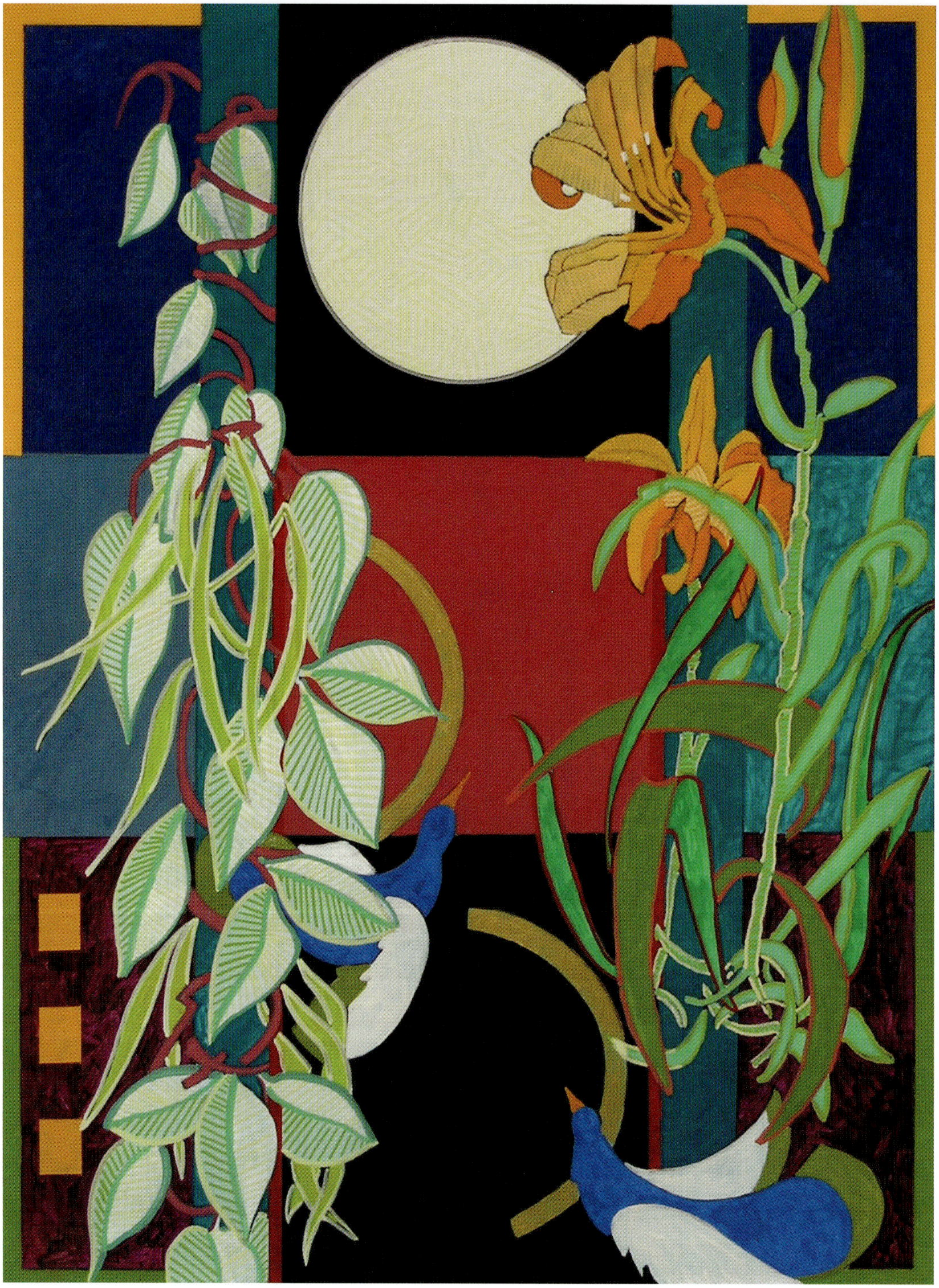

The middle way

is not so tame as it sounds.

You must be intentional.

You must keep your eye

on the moon.

Windfall

2020

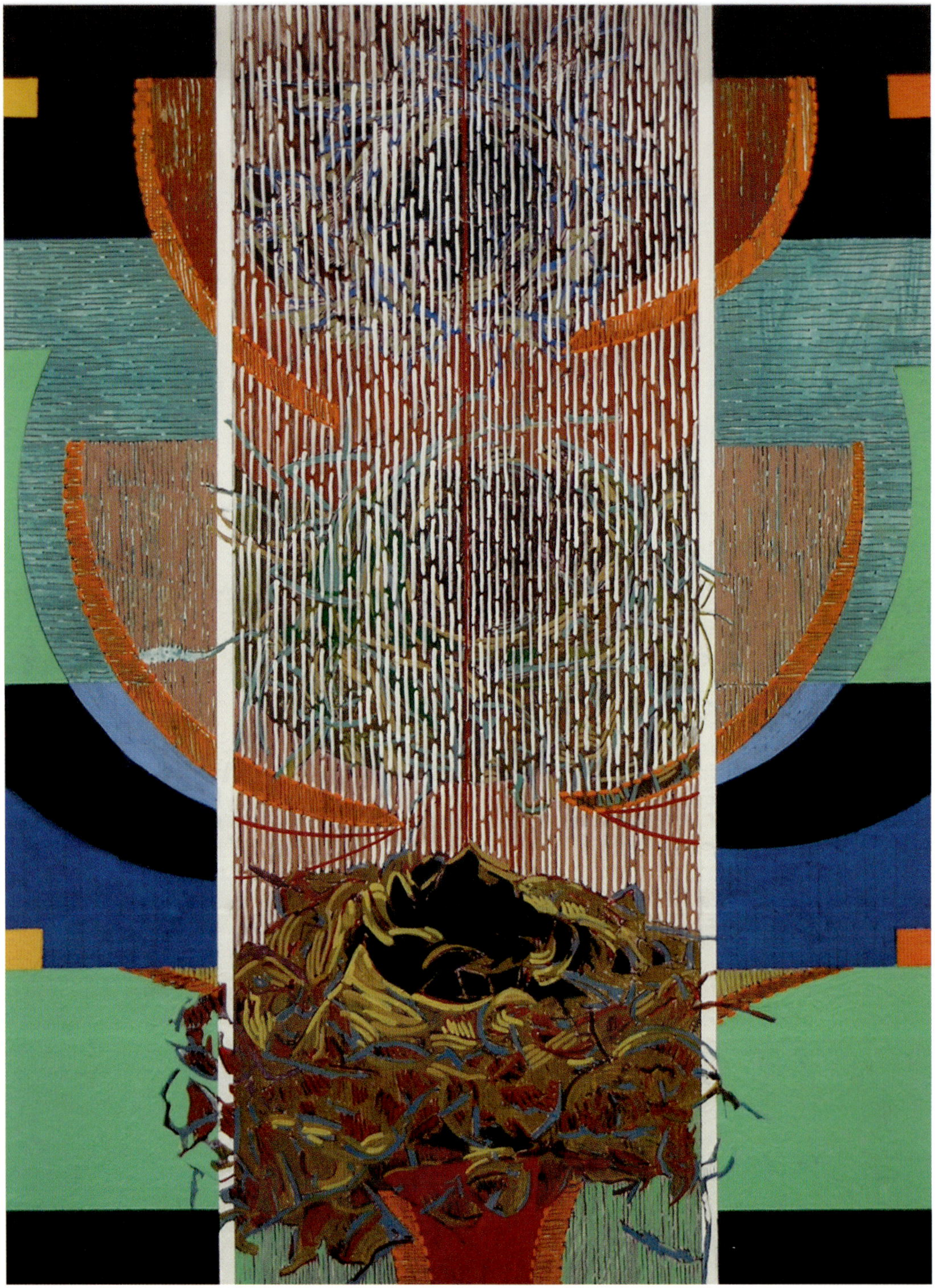

When you've had it,

just stay home.

Pet the cat. Water the plants.

Curl up with the dog if you like.

Drink warm liquids.

Eat cinnamon toast,

or maybe buttered noodles.

Gaze out the window.

Imagine the innumerable causes

that have brought about this peace.

That will be enough

for now.

Just write.

The pen dragging
over paper, leaking
ink in its track feels
just right.
There is nothing
more true than
this, now.

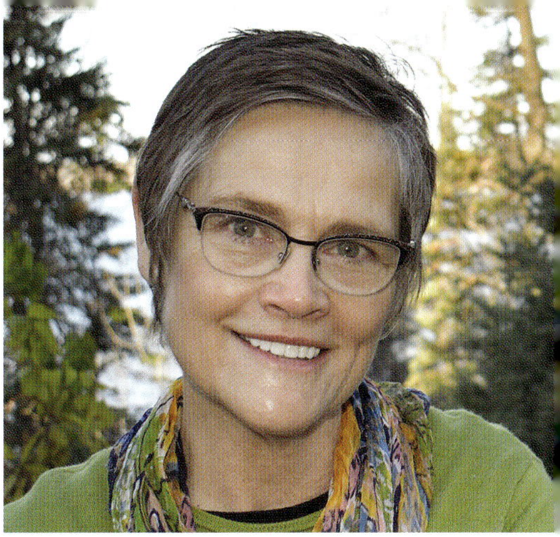

On being Taiju

In the Zen community, I am known by my dharma name, Taiju, which means Peaceful Jewel. I began my Zen training at Ryumonji Zen Monastery in 2007 and was ordained in 2015. I was the trainee whose toe repeatedly got caught in the hem of her robe; who dropped a burning ember of incense on the polished wooden floor of the Buddha Hall; who arrived in work clothes when she should have been in robes; who rang the bell at the wrong time. I worked so hard getting things right that I got them wrong. I remember wondering what had possessed my teacher when he named me Peaceful Jewel. Often I asked myself, "Where's the peace? Where's the jewel?"

I practice zazen, a form of meditation that requires being still and witnessing life as it happens, with minimal effort or resistance. This was difficult to learn because I grew up thinking my value was in acquiring, possessing, and working hard to control outcomes in my life. Zazen is the practice of stepping back from external sources of value and simply being with life as it unfolds moment by moment without judgment. This simple practice requires responding to life as it is now, but not in a passive or indifferent way.

I have come to see my purpose not as controlling but as navigating in a world that is complex and fluid. I've been taught by wise mentors to "take care of *this*, the only moment you have." Thus, every moment is worth my attention without question! Caring for life in this way is an act of respect, and leaves me saturated with gratitude.

A dharma name is significant. It is chosen carefully for the person being named, but it is not merely a descriptive label. It is bestowed as a gift, not as flattery but as a teaching. Living with this name for more than a decade, I am still discovering what it has to teach me.

Although I've read and written poetry since childhood, my recent poems are influenced by my daily observations cultivated by my meditation practice. These poems often document a moment of seeing or knowing, prior to any action or intention. Such observations may lead into action. Sometimes they stand on their own—valuable only for marking engaging or amusing moments.

Writing poetry gives rise to awareness, clarity, and joy in my life.

—Taiju Geri Wilimek

On painting

My work has arrived at a point of completion. Maturing as an artist and gaining a vocabulary of shapes always related to the land I have lived on, I end this new series of egg tempera paintings feeling very good about the results. Over the past six decades, I have completed nearly 400 works in gouache, casein, acrylic, and, with the last 120 works, egg tempera.

Painting is a discipline that requires high craft, understanding of color, and acute observation. It takes patience to continue producing a professional level of quality. Patience is cultivated by doing the work and doing it over if it doesn't measure up.

Egg tempera is an ancient painting medium that demands craft be properly applied. It does not easily forgive. I like the intimacy of the process . . . a good drawing to start with, a properly charged brush, and a gradual accumulation of brushstrokes. The strokes are not just marks: They are bits of energy. The intensity of my energy, the speed of my energy, and the anxiety of my energy. It's a slow endeavor, beginning with developing a color theory, then drying time in between layers of paint, scraping off mistakes, and framing the painting for public viewing.

My poet friend Geri introduced me to Zen Buddhism. Sitting meditation is an asset for

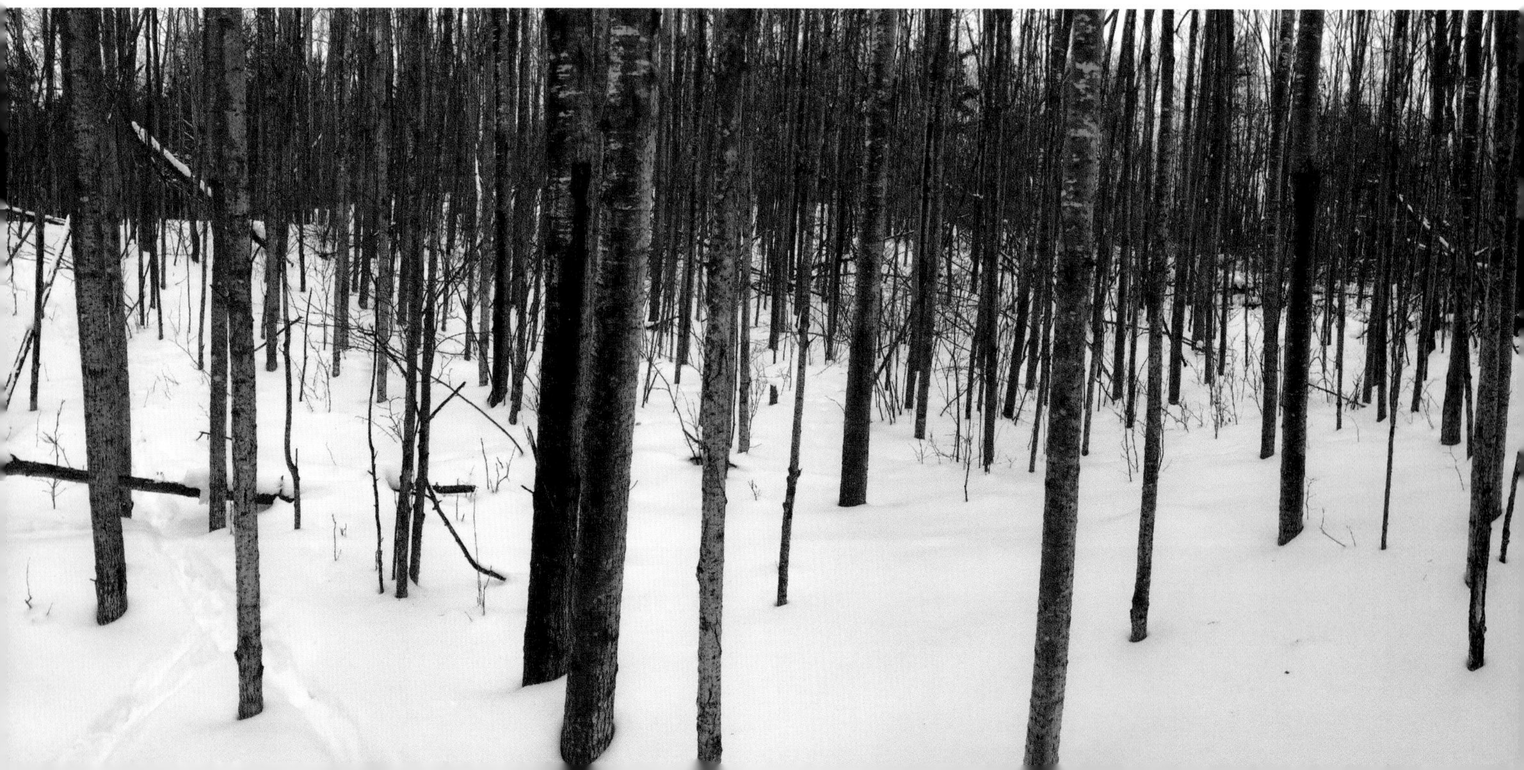

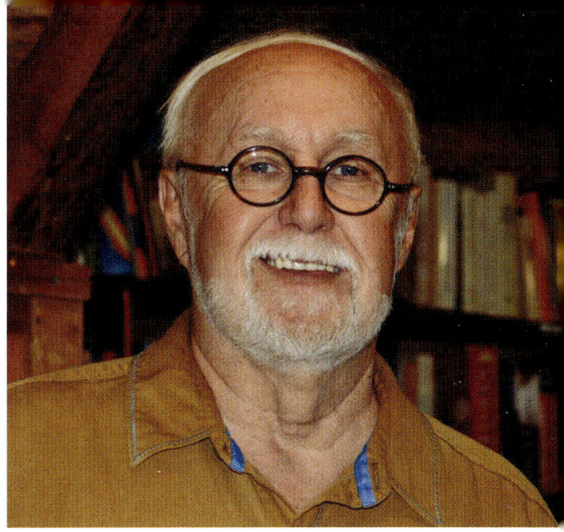

me. It allows me to slow down and lets the brushstrokes come to me. Much of my work process is done alone, seated at a table, without sound, within a comfortable environment. There is adequate light. There are large display areas, and rarely are there visitors. All of this lends itself to a meditative environment.

Some years ago, I was diagnosed with a rare medical condition, pulmonary fibrosis. I was just finishing my first book, *Letters to Isabella*, which included 77 egg tempera paintings and a letter to my granddaughter Isabella about each one. Art critic Mary Abbe of the *Star Tribune* called it "A Book of Love," and it was.

Geri came calling when she heard of my health issue. We talked about meditation and how I was using it. At that point I was on oxygen full-time, tethered to an oxygen-concentrator machine in my studio, my house, and anywhere I went. Given my physical limitations, I decided to do a series of

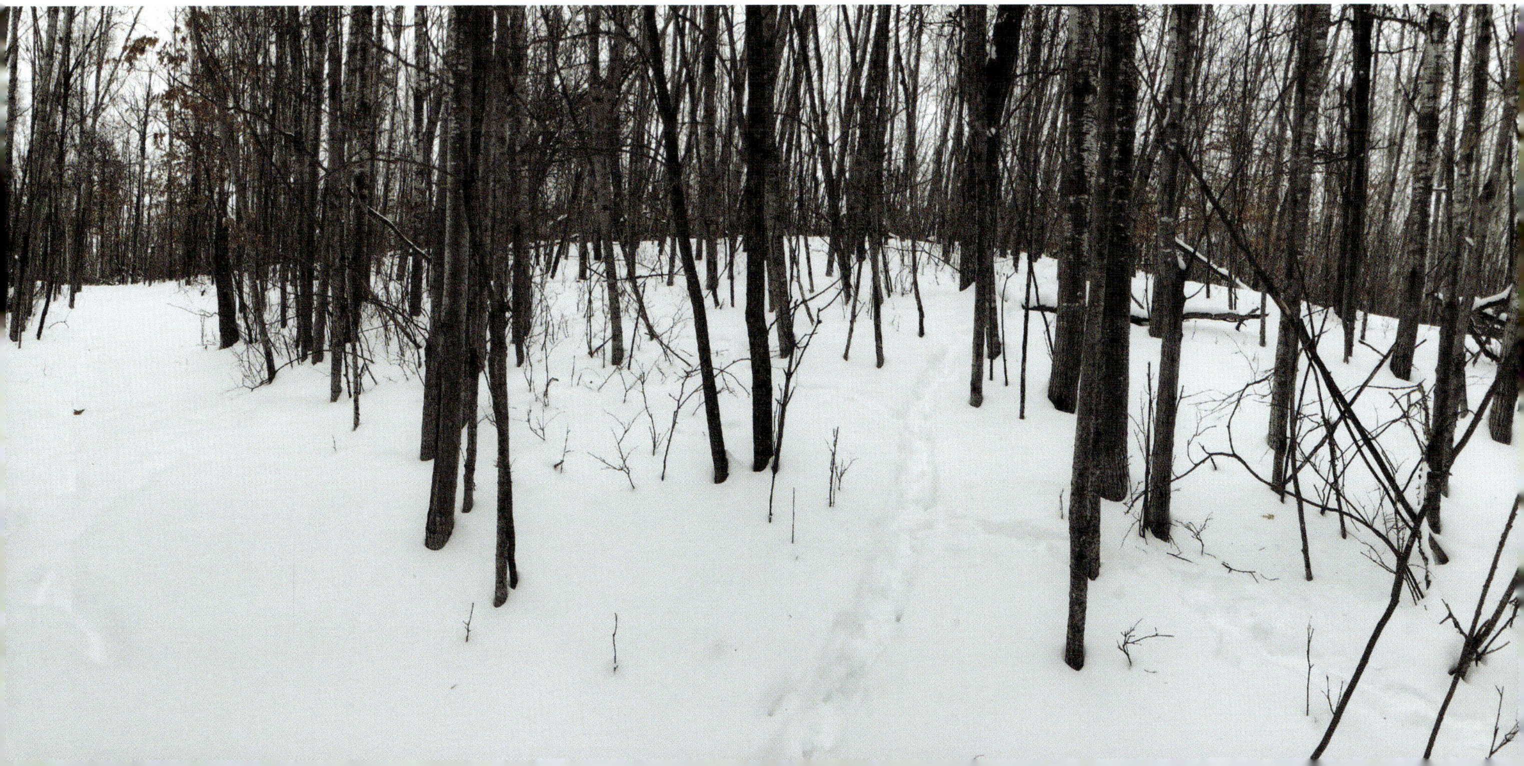

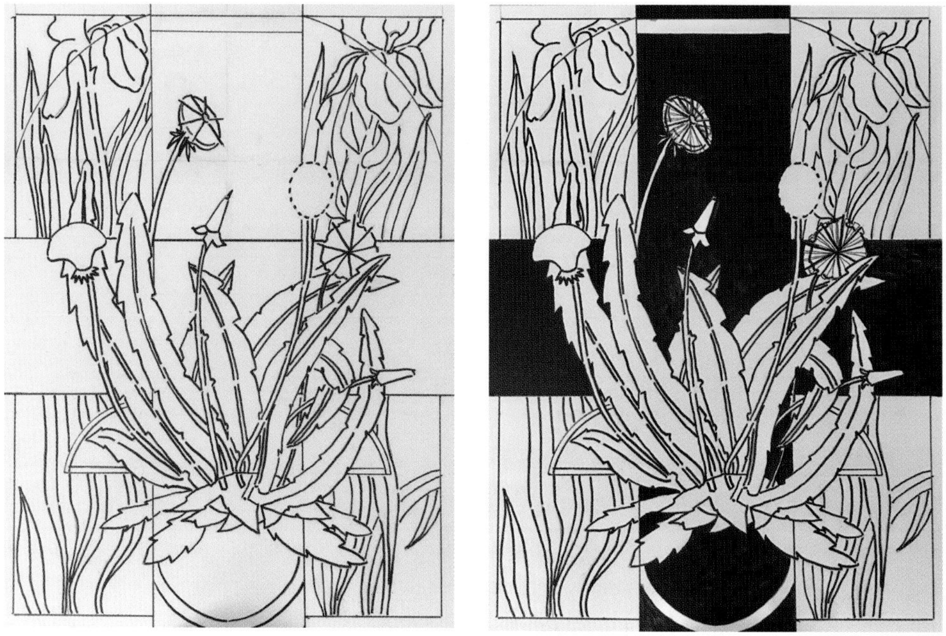

Artist's study of dandelions and pen-and-ink pre-drawing on panel for egg tempera painting First Bouquet, *page 10.*

smaller works based on clear parameters.

Like icons painted in Eastern and Western cultures to enhance certain religious environments, my egg tempera paintings are small and intended to accommodate one viewer at a time. This privacy of viewing is a way to allow the reaction to be personal.

During our conversations, Geri and I decided to produce a book together. That book, *We Sit*, published in 2018, included 20 of my painting images and 20 of Geri's poems. Those pieces were not meant to be about each other, as we had worked independently; but paired in the book, they attained an unanticipated harmony. My hope is that our collaboration on *For Now* achieves similar harmony for the reader.

Most of my images derive from commonplace things. I utilize metaphor and build the painting by giving weight to myth, ancient and contemporary thought found in literature, and other visual images. The finished painting often reveals, to me, the otherwise unknowable. My work has become a kind of meditation art. Is this meditative practice a struggle or a blessing? For now, it's both. The struggle is a regular waning of energy to work. The blessing comes when the visual choices of design and color solidify and give me satisfaction to go on.

At this time in my life, I have a better understanding of who I really am. I am a man in my 80s who grew up in a rural farm home. In college I was trained to be a painter. I have learned to see, create, and design with images in and about the land where I live.

The land and all its inhabitants are my subjects; they elicit wonder and surprise as I compose and structure on a two-dimensional format. One critic said I was "farming with color." Another noted that "the brushstrokes became a meditative means to build rhythm, balance and encourage seeing in the moment." My interest in Buddhist philosophy is directly related to how I see, evaluate, and develop meaning.

—Marley Kaul

Paintings

Egg tempera on panels, each 16 inches by 12 inches.

POEMS